# Kiss the Frog

## Integrating and Transforming Your Business with BPI

By Richard Schultz

Published by Aspatore, Inc.

Please help us make this book better by emailing us corrections, updates, comments or any other inquiries at info@aspatore.com.

First Printing, 2003
10 9 8 7 6 5 4 3 2 1

Copyright © 2003 by Aspatore, Inc. All rights reserved. Printed in the United States of America. No part of this publication may be reproduced or distributed in any form or by any means, or stored in a database or retrieval system, except as permitted under Sections 107 or 108 of the United States Copyright Act, without prior written permission of the publisher.

ISBN 1-58762-351-X

Cover design by Traci Whitney

Edited by Lance Tatro

Material in this book is for informational purposes only.

This book is printed on acid free paper.

A special thanks to all the individuals that made this book possible.

To my boys, Trevor and Parker, and my wife Stacey, who is still waiting for me to turn into a prince.

Jim,

Thank you for your continued support. I appreciate your coaching and guidance, we are looking forward to mutual successes!

# Kiss the Frog

## Table of Contents

| | |
|---|---|
| Preface | 7 |
| Chapter 1: The Frog Prince | 11 |
| Chapter 2: Delivering Business Solutions | 21 |
| Chapter 3: Traditional Approaches to Integration | 33 |
| Chapter 4: The Myths of Integration | 47 |
| Chapter 5: The Top-down Approach to Integration | 53 |
| Chapter 6: The Continuously Evolving Business | 65 |
| Chapter 7: The Bottom Line: Return On Investment | 77 |
| Chapter 8: Will the Real BPI Please Stand Up? | 87 |
| Chapter 9: Preparing for the Future | 103 |
| Glossary | 109 |
| Author's Biography | |

# Preface

## Richard Schultz

As far back as I can remember, I have gravitated toward solving problems – not just any problems, but truly taxing ones, like learning Beethoven's entire *Moonlight Sonata* on the piano at a young age, taking computer science courses at Yale when I was still in high school, and trying to prove $P$ is not equal to $NP$.

Granted, many challenges have been beyond my grasp. Over time, however, I have honed my ability to select endeavors that come very close to that "impossible" status, yet are achievable. One of those opportunities, integration, first crossed my path years ago, while I was working with companies in financial services, manufacturing, and energy.

Here was a problem that *had* to be solved for companies to leverage the Internet and their existing IT assets. The goals of integration were clear: better service, cost reduction, and a flexible infrastructure that adapts quickly to changing business requirements. But the only existing solutions involved complex network technology and extensive consulting engagements, and the solutions still came far short of satisfying the goals.

Being able to adapt business systems as business processes change is becoming a paramount objective, but business process integration (BPI) is not an entirely new concept. Rather, it is a combination and an evolution of solutions in related disciplines. For example, in the networking world, people built networks before routers existed. They were extremely customized, very hard to scale, and considered an option for only the largest organizations. The development of the router enabled a discontinuity in the market regarding how networking was applied and, in fact, was the catalyst for the Internet itself.

This book focuses on BPI and its ability to leverage computing systems and business processes. It's not all pretty: Integration is generally described as one of the ugliest undertakings an organization can face. But effective techniques for BPI exist today, and I have tried to lend some perspective on the problems businesses encounter, why they are so difficult to tackle, and how they can be approached – and solved –

innovatively. Once you've embraced BPI, you'll find that the results can be remarkable. Go ahead: Kiss the frog.

Richard Schultz
New Haven, Connecticut

# 1

# The Frog Prince

## When Wishes Come True

"Long ago, when wishes came true..." begins the famous fairy tale that eventually spawned the romantic notion of kissing an ugly frog and transforming it into a handsome prince. When it comes to computer technology, companies often have many handsome princes in the form of systems that can perform incredibly complex calculations in milliseconds or retrieve precise information from a database with millions upon millions of records. But when the computer systems are built with different types of technology, they can be a huge impediment to progress and profitability. The individual technology assets on their own may be dazzlingly impressive, but if the company can't make the systems work together to achieve important business goals, the overall IT environment is more likely to resemble the ugly frog of folklore than any prince.

Today the leaders of almost every major company wrestle with some type of integration problem and advocate the benefits of tying together the company's systems. So what do today's C-level executives wish for? They want to harness the power of *all* their computer systems, and that means coordinating their interaction when a particular business process cannot be completed by one system alone.

To be sure, turning ugliness into beauty sounds like a lofty goal. In this book, we'll explain how new software known as BPI is facilitating the transformation of IT environments in all types of industries throughout the business world.

*Business process integration* – what is it? How do you know when your organization needs it? Let's explore the BPI possibilities.

## BPI: The Swiss Army Knife of Integration

Business process integration falls under the broad umbrella of integration technology. The term "integration" comes from the Latin word *integer*, meaning whole or entire. In the business world, integration technology generally refers to the methods and tools a company uses to coordinate or tie together its applications and databases, particularly when these resources are developed with different technologies and are incompatible from a processing standpoint.

Technology talk is notorious for what are jokingly referred to as TLAs (three-letter acronyms), and integration technology is no exception. In this book we'll discuss many other integration-related TLAs, such as BPM (business process management), EAI (enterprise application integration), and BAM (business activity monitoring). We've included a brief glossary at the end of the book to help alleviate confusion, but it is worth noting that many of these terms have been redefined several times in the past few years, and even today, some of the definitions are different, depending on whom you ask.

Despite the intimidating technology buzzwords, it is not necessary to be a technology expert to understand BPI; in fact, BPI is greatly simplifying the integration world. Putting aside differences of opinion among industry analysts, we can safely say that the aim of integration technology is to cope with the challenge of working with incompatible systems, inside and outside the company. If each computer system is a piece of the IT puzzle that functions well on its own, BPI is the glue that ultimately holds the puzzle together and allows the pieces to work in harmony.

BPI is a specific form of integration technology that allows companies to focus on automating *business processes*, which we define as multi-step activities that interact with multiple systems and usually include business logic. These processes can also include human interaction. A customer or user may kick off the processes themselves through a conventional user interface, such as a company's Web site, or the processes may run behind the scenes without being initiated by any human activity.

The most distinguishable feature of BPI software is its graphical modeling environment, which allows business analysts, without writing code, to create visual representations of the business processes being automated. In addition, what makes BPI a unique approach to integration is that it is a *single, unified software package* containing all the capabilities needed to solve the vast majority of integration problems. This is in direct contrast to other approaches to integration technology

> **BPI is a single, unified package containing all the capabilities needed to solve the vast majority of integration problems.**

that provide highly specialized solutions or require the coordination of many different components. It may help to think of BPI as the Swiss army knife of integration – there are times when you might need a chef's knife or other specialized piece of equipment, but for everyday chores, the Swiss army knife is a more practical, cost-effective, and easy-to-use tool.

### Integration and Customer Service

When a customer phones a company's call center, the customer service representatives (CSRs) might need access to customer-specific details (name, address, and order history, for example), as well as more general information (such as inventory levels, shipping data, or product availability dates). If the customer service reps are forced to look up customer information in one application and product details in another, the time spent on the call increases, and the level of service suffers. In most call centers this also creates a ripple effect, as other callers in the queue spend more time on hold, waiting for a representative.

If the call center's systems were integrated, the customer service representatives would have a means to view information from all the pertinent systems in one place. Ideally, the representatives would not even be aware that the Web page or screen they were viewing contained data that was pulled together from multiple systems or databases, since

# Kiss the Frog

from a user's perspective this is irrelevant. With the caller on the line, the CSRs could quickly:

- Take the customer's order for new merchandise
- Check the availability of the desired products
- Provide the shipping details, including a tracking number
- Offer a selection of promotional products based on the customer's profile

Fully integrated systems would also allow the company to offer self-service. Customers who did not wish to use the phone could simply place their orders by visiting the company's Web site.

For a more specific example of the kinds of improvements integration can make possible, we will look at the first of four case studies, all of which are based on actual BPI implementations. In this first case study we've omitted some implementation details in favor of a high-level overview of the business problem and integration solution, but later in the book we will take a more detailed look at other successful BPI projects.

## Case Study: Consolidating Bill Payments

> *A classic candidate for an integration solution, Peoples Telecommunication Company (PTC) provides landline and wireless service to its customers, but it has separate systems to administer these two types of services. When it was time to apply bill payments, customer service representatives did not have what is frequently referred to in the industry as a "customer 360° view." In other words, they could not access all customer information from one system. If a customer had two accounts, the CSRs had to enter a significant amount of information twice, even if the customer had sent in a single payment for both accounts.*

15

*Slowing the process even more was the CSRs' need to access multiple computer screens to process one payment.*

## Inefficient Customer Service

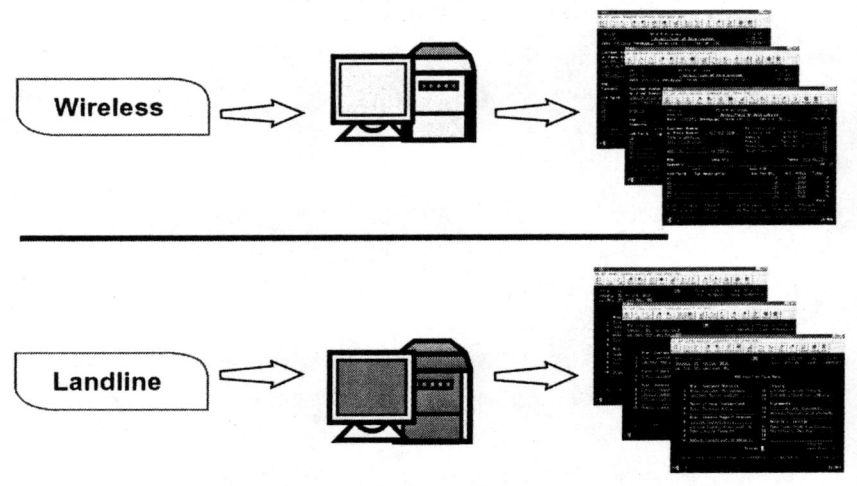

**Separate Account Handling for Wireless and Landline**

      Both billing systems performed valuable functionality, so gutting these applications and building a new system did not make sense. The company wanted a quick, inexpensive solution that would combine the functionality of its two existing billing systems and drastically reduce the time CSRs spent handling payments. This ability to quickly assemble new business processes by gluing together existing functionality from different systems is one of the core benefits of BPI.

# Customer 360° Solutions

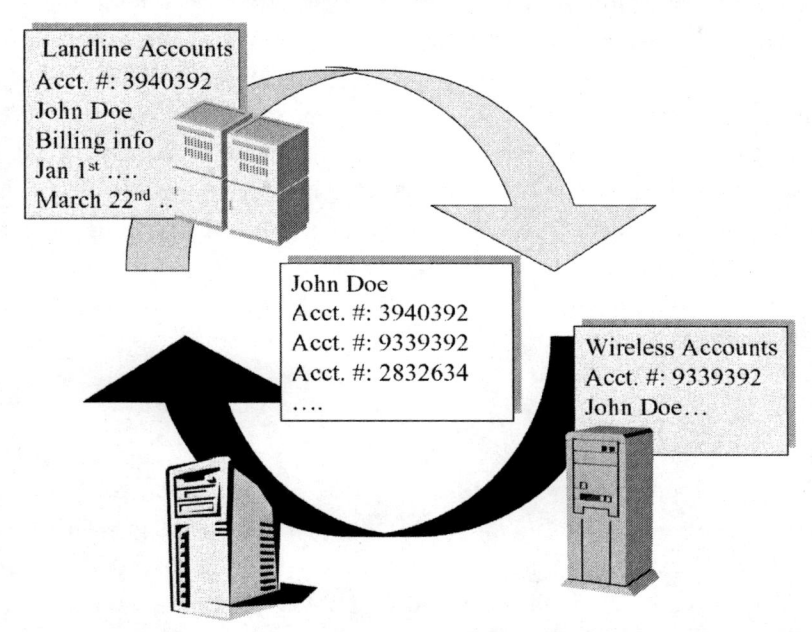

Landline Accounts
Acct. #: 3940392
John Doe
Billing info
Jan 1st ....
March 22nd ..

John Doe
Acct. #: 3940392
Acct. #: 9339392
Acct. #: 2832634
....

Wireless Accounts
Acct. #: 9339392
John Doe...

In just two weeks, PTC used BPI software to power a Web interface that interacted with the incompatible billing systems. The CSRs could now enter the customer information – once – along with the amount being paid, and both systems were updated to reflect the payment.

With its BPI solution, the staff no longer has to be trained on two different legacy billing systems and instead can use one simple Web interface. CSRs now spend significantly less time on each customer transaction, and the level of customer service has improved tremendously.

In today's competitive market, almost every enterprise needs integration technology. In fact, it's easier to identify those that don't need integration. Unless the company runs its business with a single software application, chances are the company will benefit from tying together data and functionality from multiple systems. The need extends across all industries: retail, telecommunications, financial services, healthcare, manufacturing, transportation, government, and so on.

Typically, the larger the corporation, the more obvious is its need for integration. But mid-market companies and smaller organizations need integration, too. Most large corporations have been involved in integration efforts for some time, but many smaller companies have also begun to realize integration is critical to their well-being. Until recently, the cost of integration projects and the technology expertise required to implement them were beyond the grasp of all but the largest corporations.

**The Moore the Merrier**

Gordon Moore was one of the founders of Intel. One of his early observations in the mid-1960s was about the expected growth of the number of transistors that could fit on a chip. He predicted that every eighteen months the industry would find a way to double the number of transistors on a chip. Although Moore's original four-page paper on this topic has been interpreted in a variety of ways, he was essentially forecasting that the mass production of chips would result in continual, exponential improvements, which would in turn lead to similar leaps in productivity by the people harnessing this computer power.

Moore turned out to be right about these integrated circuits, and his theory has been successfully applied to processors, networks, and more recently even to such items such as cell phones and DVD players. Moore's Law has been applied very broadly, and it tends to hold up.

# Graph from Moore's Original Paper

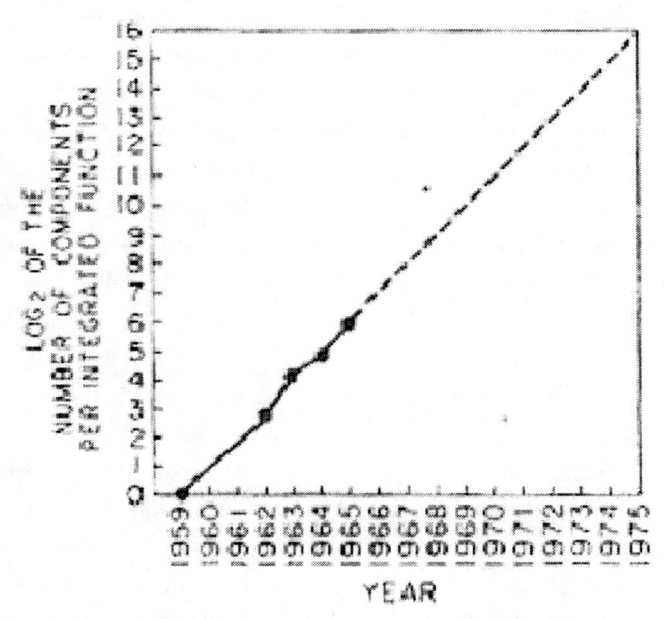

*[Graph: Log₂ of the number of components per integrated function vs. Year (1959–1975), showing a linear increase.]*

But interestingly, until the introduction of BPI, the world of integration did not show the kinds of productivity increases that we have seen with other technology. Ten years ago it took a couple of years and millions of dollars to complete any significant integration project. Five years ago was no different. Today integration projects can still take years and involve an enormous cash outlay – unless a company abandons the traditional approach in favor of BPI.

Why hasn't Moore's Law applied to integration? A close examination of the industry reveals that there has never been a single integration technology that could be commoditized and continually refined. We have seen custom coding, attempts to hardwire systems together, and companies that have undertaken the daunting task of building an infrastructure, but there has been no unified software package capable of addressing the bulk of a company's integration requirements. It isn't so surprising, then, that it has taken so long to accelerate the pace of integration projects.

BPI is a packaged software product, and that changes things. The difference between BPI and traditional integration technology is similar to the difference between hiring a carpenter to build a bookcase and going to Home Depot to buy a bookcase-building package that includes a set of tools and a step-by-step assembly guide. Everyone who buys the package gets the same set of tools and the same instructions. Furthermore, unlike hiring a carpenter, there is no doubt about what the finished product will look like. (Of course, this example assumes that the Home Depot patron or someone in the household knows how to use tools in the first place!)

With new capabilities continually being added to the BPI package (such as more connectors and pre-built process models, which we will discuss in more detail later), and more and more case studies being published describing comprehensive BPI projects that have been completed in three- or four-month timeframes, signs are starting to emerge that integration technology will begin to conform to Moore's law, at least for the next several years.

Just as the increased speed in computer chips has paved the way for massive and widespread productivity improvements around the globe, the introduction of packaged BPI software, based on an underlying engine capable of coordinating activities that are executed on multiple computer applications, gives companies a set of tools that will have a direct effect on metrics, such as how long it takes to complete integration projects and how quickly people can learn how to use the software.

# 2

# Delivering Business Solutions

## Opportunities for Integration

Well before the advent of BPI and even before the Internet explosion, many companies recognized that integration technology was the key to running a successful business. The capabilities that the Internet now offers, combined with a troubled economy and a landscape that has never been more competitive, have only intensified the need for integration. Business agility and bottom-line growth are paramount. Companies are expected to address new market demands or introduce new partner services or products into automated processes, and they need to do it in days or weeks, rather than in months or years.

Companies may have a tendency to think more in terms of business solutions today than in the past, but their objectives are still the same: gain a competitive edge, improve service, increase revenue opportunities, reduce operating costs, and in general, do business more efficiently. Companies can meet these objectives by using integration technology to roll out any of the following solutions:

- **Supply Chain Management (SCM) solutions:** Supply chain management is defined as the coordination of materials, information, and finances as they move in a process from supplier to manufacturer to wholesaler to retailer to consumer. Typically, companies use integration technology to present the image of a "virtual" organization. For example, when a customer orders a book from an online bookstore's Web site, the customer's request will be honored regardless of whether the book is in stock or needs to be obtained by accessing a supplier's system. As long as customers receive the book they ordered, on the date they expect it, they do not and should not care whether the book was shipped from the "real" bookstore or from the "virtual" bookstore (in other words, by one of the bookstore's suppliers that is transparent to customers).

    In the insurance world, a different form of SCM solution is needed to help insurance carriers wrestle with the complexities of providing products to multiple independent agents who use different agency management systems and technologies. Carriers that can make business as easy as possible for independent agents have an unquestionable advantage. Integration can mean the difference between providing insurance quotes in real time and taking days to respond via fax.

## BPI Business Solutions

**Self-Service**
**Supply Chain Management**
**Compliance Initiatives**
**Customer Relationship Management**
**Enterprise Portals**

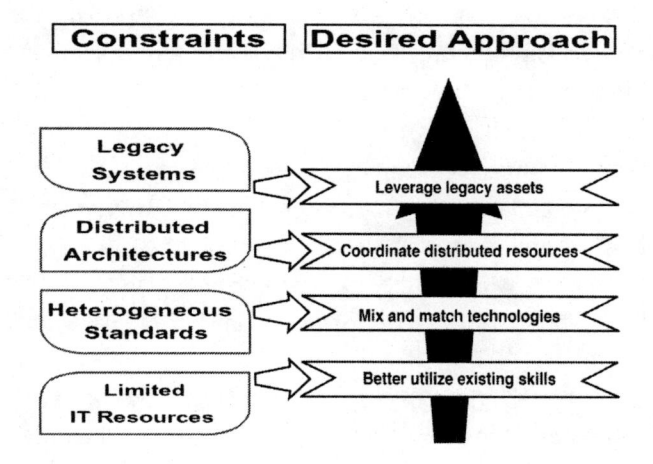

| Constraints | Desired Approach |
|---|---|
| Legacy Systems | Leverage legacy assets |
| Distributed Architectures | Coordinate distributed resources |
| Heterogeneous Standards | Mix and match technologies |
| Limited IT Resources | Better utilize existing skills |

- **Company portals:** A company's portal (not to be confused with portals such as Yahoo) offers a unified view for the visitor, but any number of systems may be contributing to the functionality the visitor sees. A well-designed, user-friendly portal can be a huge competitive edge, and BPI is an extremely effective way to tie together the systems that are working behind the scenes.

- **Customer 360° Views:** Most companies do not have full-blown CRM (Customer Relationship Management) applications, and those that do have not been able to integrate the CRM application with the other systems that drive the business. Instead of embarking on a yearlong, multi-million dollar excursion into the world of CRM, companies are discovering that BPI can help create the kind of unified customer views advertised by CRM vendors. In the insurance and financial services industry, agents are using customer profiles for specific revenue-generating opportunities, such as up-selling and cross-selling products and services, but, as we saw earlier, any company's service will be improved when customer service representatives can field calls without having to look up information in multiple systems.

- **Self-Service:** Customers are in charge today, and businesses survive and thrive by offering choice and value that customers find compelling. Today choice is not limited to a variety of products. Customers want online access to products and services that used to be available only in the office, from the store, or at the drive-thru window.

    Organizations that offer self-service solutions have been able to capture market share from larger, more established players that offer limited capabilities through a corporate Web site. Consumers and partners expect *at least* the same levels of service via the Internet as they can get through other mechanisms. For example, in the financial world, customers no longer wish to wait until the end of the month or quarter to receive detailed information about the performance of their investments. They want to be able to log on at any time. The admonition, "If you don't make your customers happy, someone else will," has never been truer than it is today.

## Self-Service BPI Case Study: Printing Truck Weight Certificates

*In many states, every truck is required by law to carry a certificate verifying its weight limits and tax ID. This document must be renewed each year and amended any time there is a significant change, such as the transfer of license plates. To issue these certificates and record the payment, the state's department of transportation (DOT) must interact with three different, incompatible sources: a mainframe database that keeps track of carrier information, an external application that processes the credit card payment, and a mainframe application that records the payment and certification details.*

*Before BPI, trucking companies had to request these certificates in person, by phone, or via e-mail or regular mail. DOT representatives spent approximately thirty minutes issuing each certificate. With more than 300,000 trucks in the state, the manual effort required to keep pace with certificate demands was staggering.*

*Like most organizations today, the DOT wanted to improve service and cut operating costs. What better way to do so than to develop a self-service solution that would allow truckers to request, pay for, and print the certificates online?*

*In a matter of weeks, the DOT rolled out its new Web site capabilities to five pilot motor carriers. After logging in with an ID and password, each carrier was able to supply the required vehicle data, along with its credit card information. When the transaction was completed, the carrier could print the certificate from the Web site.*

*The DOT quickly made several more transactions available to motor carriers, ranging from address changes to the online filing of highway use tax reports. Since many of the transactions required the trucking companies to remit payments, the same credit card functionality was reused multiple times. Just four months after the initial pilot, approximately 5,000 transactions had been processed online – with no DOT intervention. Even by the most conservative estimates, the DOT has done away with more than 5,000 hours of unnecessary labor and achieved a remarkable and rapid return on its BPI investment.*

## Responding to Unforeseen Events

Even when companies are not focused on rolling out a self-service initiative or another related, comprehensive solution, they can suddenly be thrust into a situation that demands integration technology. Compliance initiatives are an excellent example. A company with inflexible systems can face enormous setbacks when it is required to make changes to comply with new industry regulations. *In fact, this is the leading reason companies undertake IT projects in general.*[1] For instance, in the insurance industry, healthcare providers and payers are still working to comply with HIPAA (Health Insurance Portability and Accountability Act), which was introduced in 1996! Many of these entities have been forced to enlist the help of information bureaus to comply with new claims processing and patient accounting requirements, as well as many other aspects of their business.

Mergers and acquisitions can also throw a company's IT department into a state of temporary flux. Lacking an effective integration strategy, a company might find itself launching a complicated project to replace an

---

[1] C. Young, Gartner Group, "Selling IT Investments to Business Leaders," October 10, 2001.

inherited system simply because the system was built with non-standard technology or is incompatible with the rest of the company's applications. With BPI, on the other hand, companies can adapt much more quickly by automating business processes that retrieve information from the systems the company has always used, as well as from those applications it has just acquired.

Finally, some corporations are in such precarious financial positions or face such severe competitive pressure that they must find ways to reduce costs and become more efficient. Manual processes come under intense scrutiny as these struggling companies analyze the reasons for human intervention. In many cases, the manual processes exist because data from one application needs to find its way into a different system, and with no easy way to integrate its systems, the company can do little to operate more effectively.

## The Cost Without Integration

Any one of the solutions or situations described above can have a tremendous impact on a company's bottom line, and because of BPI's ability to reduce costs, the impact is especially obvious in a down economy. But in any economy, integration improves the company's effectiveness, so the question becomes a matter of urgency and opportunity. For example, a carrier that reduces the insurance quote process from two days to sixty seconds will dramatically increase the odds of getting the agent's business. In this case the cost of *not* integrating is measured not only by the cost savings that could be generated by shortening the process time, but also in lost revenue opportunity.

If the same insurance company chooses not to integrate, it also will miss out on a chance to shorten its underwriting cycle – for example, by connecting to the systems of the medical laboratories that process the applicants' blood work and the service providers that check the applicants' financial history. Perhaps the thought of eliminating faxes and other unnecessary paperwork seems attractive, though not enough for the company to pull the BPI trigger. But consider this: If a claim occurs between the time the application and initial premium are submitted and the time the underwriting decision is made, the company is legally bound to cover the claim. A company that uses BPI to reduce its underwriting process from weeks to days greatly reduces the risk of underwriting business it might not have wanted in its portfolio, and thus its claim exposure.

## Typical Insurance Issuance Process

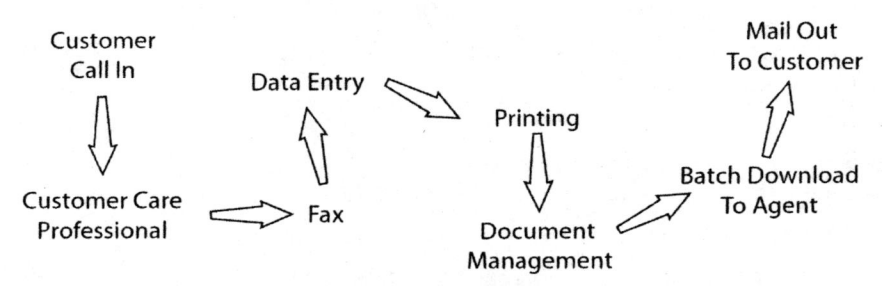

Customer Call In → Customer Care Professional → Fax → Data Entry → Printing → Document Management → Batch Download To Agent → Mail Out To Customer

But even when we remove lost revenue opportunities and potential claim exposure from the equation, chances are good that the benefits of eliminating unnecessary paperwork and faxes alone will far outweigh the cost of the BPI software for most large or mid-sized businesses that underwrite hundreds of policies each week.

### BPI and Business Process Reengineering

For years, corporations have recognized process reengineering as a way to cut costs, determine how to be more effective, and open new channels for revenue. However, business process reengineering essentially was limited to process changes. Consultants might have advised, "You'd be more effective as a company if you did things this way," but there was no technology to make the process improvements a reality. In fact, because of technology constraints, the time required to modify processes severely limited reengineering efforts and went against the reengineering notion of radical, sweeping change in the first place. Coupling the concept of reengineering processes with an integration technology solution closes this gap.

In general, we see the benefits of this kind of breakthrough only when there is a technological innovation. BPI represents one of those quantum leaps forward in the evolution of integration. Integration has been available for years – but, for all practical purposes, only to large corporations that could afford the high expense and time-consuming disruption of a custom design and build. Companies pursued integration only when they could afford it.

BPI has changed integration indelibly, and its timing could hardly be better. Companies that have identified bottlenecks from business process reengineering studies have a second chance to reexamine and clear these logjams because they can automate many more processes than ever before. The companies that for years have been saying, "Our service would be much better and quicker if we could only find a way to avoid having our representatives look up customer information in three different systems," finally have an affordable mechanism to make this goal a reality.

Even for mid-sized companies, integration is no longer a luxury, but a business imperative that is surprisingly affordable. Eventually, it will be nearly impossible for a company with more than one system to thrive – or even survive – in its marketplace without the advantages and opportunities integration provides.

## Breaking The IT Cycle

Companies have long debated the merits of centralized versus decentralized approaches to computer processing. Before the introduction of personal computers, the mainframe ran a company's applications. Most data processing took place overnight in batch. If the mainframe happened to go down, business came to a halt until the problem could be remedied.

Soon there were desktop computers and the excitement of an entirely new approach to data processing. Many companies abandoned mainframe application development in favor of client-server technology. As more and more desktop applications were rolled out, users found their ingenuity could result in important contributions to the business.

Despite zealous proclamations that the mainframe was dead, it soon became apparent that the decentralized approach was not without drawbacks. Desktop applications were far less reliable than the mainframe ever was, and companies with multiple client-server systems began to experience the first pains of the lack of integration.

The debate raged on, and the cycle continued. Centralized mid-range servers, such as the AS400s, were introduced and added to the IT manager's dilemma. ERP (Enterprise Resource Planning) solutions like SAP and PeopleSoft also clouded the landscape as organizations began to reconsider the benefits of putting everything back onto one system. Company infighting was common as the company decided whether it should buy more PCs or focus on the mainframe. It was not for some time that corporations began to realize that hardware was not the root of the problem. In the meantime some IT organizations became obsessed with getting off the mainframe, citing such issues as the lack of scalability, while mainframe advocates just as vehemently pointed to the costs and complexities of maintaining distributed systems.

## The Historical IT Cycle

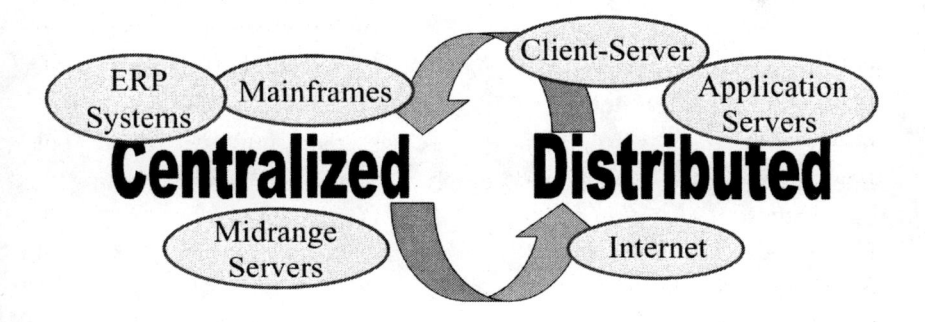

**Centralized** ⇄ **Distributed**

- ERP Systems
- Mainframes
- Midrange Servers

- Client-Server
- Application Servers
- Internet

The Internet evolution has helped companies understand that it is crucial to offer the best of both worlds: the management of a centralized resource paired with the flexibility, capability, and pricing of a distributed client-server environment. When a company rolls out functionality on its Web site, users can get the look and feel of a single system that does everything, regardless of the number of back-end systems that contribute to the site's functionality. In this way, BPI is changing the way companies think about computing and infrastructure. BPI has the potential to break the cycle – once and for all – of trying to settle on a centralized or decentralized approach.

The concepts behind BPI are not new, but what is new is the introduction of a packaged software product that companies can use to develop integration solutions quickly and without adding staff or enlisting the help of highly paid consultants. In the networking world, we saw a similar technology advancement that revolutionized the industry. When companies started building networks, system connections were hardwired. Companies would either wire all of their systems into a centralized unit, or create operational chaos as they attempted to wire together a completely distributed system. Cisco was able to combine these two models by using its router technology to provide a flexible solution that has solved the vast majority of the routing issues faced by companies today. More importantly, Cisco packaged its solution in a "box" and ensured that any company could figure out how to use it. In the software world, there has been no solution analogous to what Cisco did for hardware – until now. There were successful integration technology projects before BPI, just as there were networks before Cisco, but both of these technology solutions were limited to a strict minority of highly advanced companies. Businesses that formerly ruled out integration projects because of complexity and cost are beginning to view BPI as "integration for the rest of us."

# 3

# Traditional Approaches to Integration

## Building the Phone Company

As children, we used to play "Telephone" by taking two cans and wiring them together with string. But if several children want to build phones and talk to each other, stringing cans together quickly gets complicated, and the telephone game doesn't work so well.

## Point-to-Point Solutions

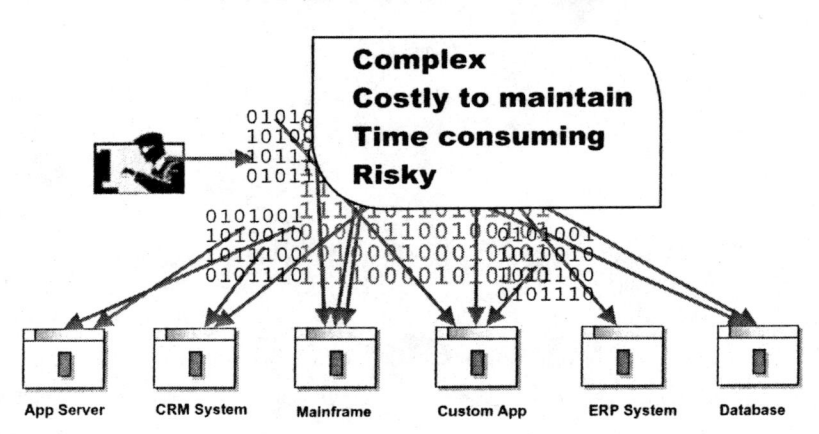

**Complex**
**Costly to maintain**
**Time consuming**
**Risky**

App Server | CRM System | Mainframe | Custom App | ERP System | Database

It's a simple analogy, but one that helps shed light on some of the problems that have long plagued traditional integration efforts. In the past, many businesses have attempted to build "point-to-point" solutions to achieve integration. In other words, when a company needed to integrate functionality from two systems, it hardwired the two applications together by writing custom code that connected one touch point to another. Once the applications could communicate with each other, developers then wrote additional custom code, often executing it on an application server to automate the desired business processes.

When companies need to integrate only two incompatible systems, point-to-point solutions can be applied. Developers can write code to automate business processes involving two disparate applications without necessarily turning the entire IT environment inside out.

## Kiss the Frog

However, as the company grows and a third system is added to the mix, the integration project becomes disproportionately complex, moves at a far slower pace, and causes a significant strain on IT resources. Bring in a fourth application, or factor in the complications of interacting outside the firewall with a business partner or supplier, and soon the integration project will spiral out of control.

It is easy to see why point-to-point solutions can cause organizations to lose sight of the business functionality they are attempting to automate. Companies can spend so much time grappling with application-level integration details that the business benefits of the project become obscured. Another serious drawback to this approach is the lack of reusability, since by definition the custom programs can be applied only to the two points being connected. *This inability to reuse functionality directly impedes the path to scalability.* Finally, once the point-to-point solution is in place, maintaining the environment and responding to future business requirements can be problematic because the business logic often is buried in hundreds of lines of custom code.

Returning for a moment to the tin-can telephone analogy, it is the lack of an underlying infrastructure that makes giving a dozen children a set of cans and some string impractical at best. In the real world, the telephone company provides the infrastructure to make this type of communication possible. Once the telephone company is built, it doesn't matter whether there are two children or two hundred; everyone can talk.

The phone company approach to integration attempts to reduce the custom-programming burden by providing an infrastructure or plumbing – most often via a message broker or bus – that connects to the underlying architecture of each disparate application in a company's technology suite. This frees companies from having to write code to connect each application but, as with point-to-point solutions, generally requires developers to write custom code to handle the business logic.

Once the infrastructure is in place, it can provide a very effective integration platform. Building an integration infrastructure addresses the scalability issue and other integration challenges, such as data

35

synchronization, quite nicely; however, it has some unfortunate correlations to the phone company example. How many people know how to build a phone company? Who has the time to build it? Or the budget to pay for it? Indeed, constructing a solid architecture that will support an entire suite of disparate, sophisticated technologies is no easy trick, which is why this type of effort historically has been outsourced to integration technology vendors. Not surprisingly, the complexity of these efforts invariably has been reflected in the cost of the projects.

In essence, creating point-to-point solutions and developing an integration infrastructure, the two most popular traditional integration approaches, involve tradeoffs. Point-to-point solutions don't require companies to build an underlying infrastructure, but these solutions don't scale well and aren't suited for large integration projects. Developing an integration infrastructure will address scalability requirements and provide a viable integration solution, but building it severely hamstrings a corporation's budget and its ability to deliver new functionality quickly because it requires a major investment of resources and time.

A few years ago a handful of the largest corporations might have been willing to invest millions of dollars and wait a year to have a consulting firm put an integration platform in place. Mid-market companies, on the other hand, have never had the budget for this type of undertaking and have had little choice except to attempt sporadic integration projects via point-to-point solutions.

Today's business demands make building an entirely new infrastructure an unpalatable course of action for most organizations, regardless of their size. Companies large and small rarely have the luxury of waiting a year before they can roll out new functionality or deliver business benefits. The competition is too fierce, and customers have too many other alternatives. And time is exactly what constructing an infrastructure requires – as the company must wait until the systems have been tied together before even *attempting* to reap business benefits by automating processes that involve incompatible systems.

## Kiss the Frog

## The CIO of the Late 1990s: Gone but Not Forgotten

Many CIOs are intimidated by the prospect of attempting enterprise-wide integration, and with a few exceptions, those who have tackled large integration projects have stories of frustration, missed deadlines, and unexpected expenses. Let's take a closer look at why infrastructure projects and point-to-point solutions have made integration so difficult for a large portion of the business world.

As we pointed out in our discussion of Moore's Law, the lack of a comprehensive software solution for integration has contributed to the general dearth of successful integration projects and sluggish growth of the industry in general. Until BPI, there has never been a single software package developed solely for integration projects. The software that was available – for messaging or data transformation, for instance – addressed pieces of the integration puzzle, but many of these pieces needed to be assembled and coordinated to achieve the larger goal of integrating the entire business.

The popular industry term for the pieces of the integration puzzle and their orchestration is the integration infrastructure stack. A typical stack is shown on the following page, although the specific layers can vary.

(We should point out that, although EAI [enterprise application integration] is shown as the part of the stack that focuses on the moving and transforming of data, the term EAI also is commonly used to refer to integration technology in general.)

## "Traditional" Integration Stack

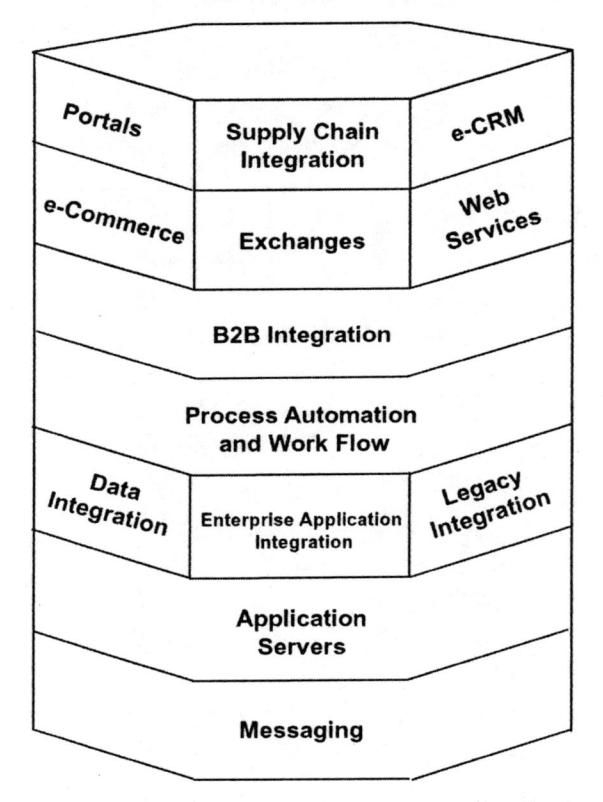

- Portals
- Supply Chain Integration
- e-CRM
- e-Commerce
- Exchanges
- Web Services
- B2B Integration
- Process Automation and Work Flow
- Data Integration
- Enterprise Application Integration
- Legacy Integration
- Application Servers
- Messaging

Instead of being armed with a single application to address integration complexities, companies have been forced to cobble together integration solutions using the technologies shown here, many of which require a high level of technical sophistication and were never intended to be particularly user-friendly. Not only did corporations need to get rapidly up to speed on application servers, messaging technology, and data integration tools, which involved significant training costs, but they also needed to figure out how to make the pieces of the stack work together.

It was not uncommon for a business to bring in a new CIO to integrate the company's systems and build an architecture that would facilitate the rolling out of integration projects. In most cases this entailed an ambitious two- or three-year plan that involved assembling the infrastructure stack and settling on a particular standard or set of standards aimed at easing future application development.

In the early days of integration, the economy was booming, and so was the consulting business. Literally thousands of consultants were deployed on large-scale integration projects across the globe, because most organizations did not have enough in-house resources with the technical skills to work with the complex set of tools required to build an infrastructure stack.

More often than not, this heavy reliance on consultants exacerbated an already difficult task. As with any group of employees, consultants have varying skill levels. Screening dozens of consultants individually is impractical, especially when the work being contracted generally is beyond the technical grasp of the hiring manager, or involves the nuts-and-bolts of application servers or proprietary middleware. The situation is not very different from someone who hires a plumber or other skilled laborer to work on his house. If the plumber says there is a problem with the backwater valve that may cause the sewers to back up during heavy rainfall, chances are the homeowner will trust this assessment because he lacks the expertise to dispute it. In fact, it's probably safe to say that a good number of people would not even be able to locate their backwater valve!

As a result, organizations ended up with consulting teams of various abilities who were hired to build the integration stack and implement new standards. In essence, they were asked to "build the phone company," even though building a phone company was not always in the business's best interest. Meanwhile, the gulf widened between the businesspeople and IT staff. The businesspeople understandably were focused on rolling out new business functionality or enhancing user experiences; therefore, the most beautifully constructed IT stack meant little to them unless it resulted in direct, tangible improvements to existing business processes. Unfortunately, in most cases, business owners were told their projects would have to wait until the magical infrastructure was in place.

This type of consultant-led integration infrastructure project typically lasted at least two years and cost companies an average of between $4 million and $6 million, and often the so-called finished product fell far short of the lofty goals set forth at the beginning of the project. (Today the annual average is $6.3 million for Global 3500 companies, so it's clear that this type of pain still exists.) It's also interesting to note that in recent years, the average CIO tenure has been rather fleeting – between fourteen and sixteen months.[2] More than one company saw a new CIO arrive, propose an impressive two-year strategy, and hire a cadre of consultants, only to accept a new position eighteen months later, leaving the company with millions of dollars in bills and consultants still hard at work building an infrastructure.

## Waiting for the Dam to Burst

Companies that shied away from building an entire integration stack in favor of point-to-point solutions faced slightly different obstacles but fared no better. As we saw earlier, this approach generally centered on making two particular systems "talk to each other," without consideration for the bigger integration picture or the long-term effects of the short-term solution.

Companies that opted for this approach may not have been as reliant on consultants, but unlike companies who successfully built their own

---

[2] Russ Banham, "Do CFOs and CIOs Need a Mediator?" *CFO Magazine,* March 2003.

## Kiss the Frog

stack, these organizations could never hope to get to a stage when projects would get progressively easier. In fact, the opposite was true. The more custom coding a company did, the larger the mess the next round of integration became.

Business and IT collaboration was not much better, either. Although business analysts did not necessarily have to wait for an entire infrastructure before business initiatives involving multiple systems could be undertaken, there were still severe limitations and a lack of shared priorities. The business experts could not drive the projects, in many cases, because they were handcuffed by the system incompatibilities and could roll out functionality only where developers had cleared the path. Frustration and miscommunication were rampant, especially when custom code was involved; many businesspeople felt the developers did not understand company priorities, and many developers felt that the businesspeople grossly underestimated the complexities of integration. It often took so long to write the code that glued two systems together that the business requirements had changed by the time the developer was supposedly done. In other cases, missing functionality was not discovered until the project had entered the testing phase.

Some organizations were able to accomplish small-scale integration projects but inevitably found that larger efforts could not be accomplished with point-to-point solutions. As more and more islands of programs and processes were built, it became increasingly difficult to weave them into the fabric of the organization. And with no underlying infrastructure to support high-availability features and tie together disparate systems, the IT environment was not unlike the story of the boy who put his fingers in the dyke to prevent a flood. Companies can plug integration holes with custom code for a little while, but eventually the river will overflow, and all the custom code in the world will be of little use.

## Checking IT Baggage

How does a company recognize when its goals cannot be achieved by conventional application development? And, once the company determines it needs integration technology, how does it know whether it should consider BPI as opposed to a point-to-point solution, an entire infrastructure stack, or a highly specialized integration tool?

As we've discussed, a company does not need to consider integration if it runs its business with a single computer system. But assuming the company has multiple applications, there are many telltale signs that should alert its decision-makers to the need for integration technology:

- *Systems have been built with different standards over time.* Applications that "don't talk to each other" stand directly in the path of straight-through processing. The company may have a clear vision when it comes to technology standards and may have settled on J2EE, for example. But what does the company do with its legacy systems, and how does it deal with partner technology that is not J2EE-compliant?

- *Data is represented differently throughout the company.* Business processes require business data. When the data is not in a universal format, real-time processes give way to manual data entry, batch conversion jobs, or other measures to transform the data into the desired format.

- *External business partners and vendors need to interact with company systems.* Many in-house systems were not designed to consider external connectivity; they present unique challenges when they become part of a business process that can be invoked by external users. In most cases companies will not want to give partners direct access to green screens, for example, even though they want to allow access to processes that expose critical business functionality.

- *Middleware or messaging technology exists, but there is no comprehensive enterprise architecture.* Middleware and messaging technology are important infrastructure components, but they do not provide the logic to run a business process and lack many other capabilities needed for full-blown development efforts.

- *Some systems are not fully fault-tolerant and have limited error-handling capabilities.* Many business applications were not designed to be fully fault-tolerant. (A fault-tolerant application is one that is configured to withstand the failure of a particular machine – for example, due to a loss of power.) However, when these applications are needed as part of an automated process that includes interaction with other systems, fault tolerance and reliability become paramount, and there is no easy way to achieve this without integration. In addition, when multiple systems are involved in a business process, the potential for errors increases, but many systems are not designed to include a sophisticated error-handling mechanism.

- *The company uses third-party systems or legacy applications over which it has no control.* If the company relies on third-party or legacy applications, it has little or no flexibility in shaping the desired business processes to meet new and changing business requirements unless it can use BPI to apply its own business rules.

- *Robust monitoring capabilities are not the norm.* Monitoring may not have been a primary consideration when a particular application was developed, but when data or functionality from multiple applications is required as part of larger process, it is critical to be able to track each system's participation in the process.

- *Some applications cannot handle increased throughput demands.* Scalability quickly can become an issue when a system originally designed to accommodate a limited number of users or transactions participates in a new process with a significantly greater transaction volume.

These signs of IT baggage are fairly easy to identify. In fact, recognizing opportunities for integration and the technical issues that must be overcome is only a small part of the battle. Most companies *know* they need integration and want to make it a reality, but they simply don't know how to go about it and are afraid of spending millions of dollars and ending up with a half-finished project to show for their investment. With some notable exceptions, there have been very few successful full-fledged integration efforts, and in general these have been limited to large corporations with seemingly unlimited budgets. As a result, there never was a best-practice model after which companies could pattern their integration projects.

If it were not for the costs and time involved in building an infrastructure stack, it would be an attractive solution for every company, large and small. (Certainly the industry's vision is that the layers in the stack will help make companies more resilient to change and make it easier to adopt new best-of-breed technologies as they are introduced, but we are somewhat skeptical that the stack of today has progressed to this point.) Ultimately, companies must consider the constraints under which they are operating. If time-to-market, a tight budget, and limited resources are key considerations, BPI clearly can be a feasible course of action.

In effect, BPI gives companies a portion – or, more precisely, a vertical slice – of the infrastructure stack. Thus, it has all the elements one would find in a traditional stack. When examining each element under the integration microscope, a company might discover that it may have particular pieces of functionality that would be better handled by a specialized tool. For this reason, a company must consider the types of projects it plans to undertake, keeping in mind the Swiss army knife analogy. In most cases the company should come to the conclusion that there is a wide variety of projects that lend themselves to integration. However, if the company has a special need to pass large volumes of data from one system to another, with very little business logic involved, it may wish to supplement its BPI software with an ETL (extract, transform, and load) tool that was designed almost exclusively for this purpose.

The graphic on the following page contrasts BPI to the integration infrastructure stack as traditional integration vendors often depict it. Note that, in the traditional view, BPI is only one of many layers in the stack. However, to undertake integration technology projects using the traditional infrastructure approach, companies need all of the layers shown here. With BPI, companies get a slice of each part of the infrastructure stack, and if they have special requirements, they can supplement the BPI software with the particular layer they need, as opposed to having to build the entire stack.

## A Vertical Slice of the Integration Stack

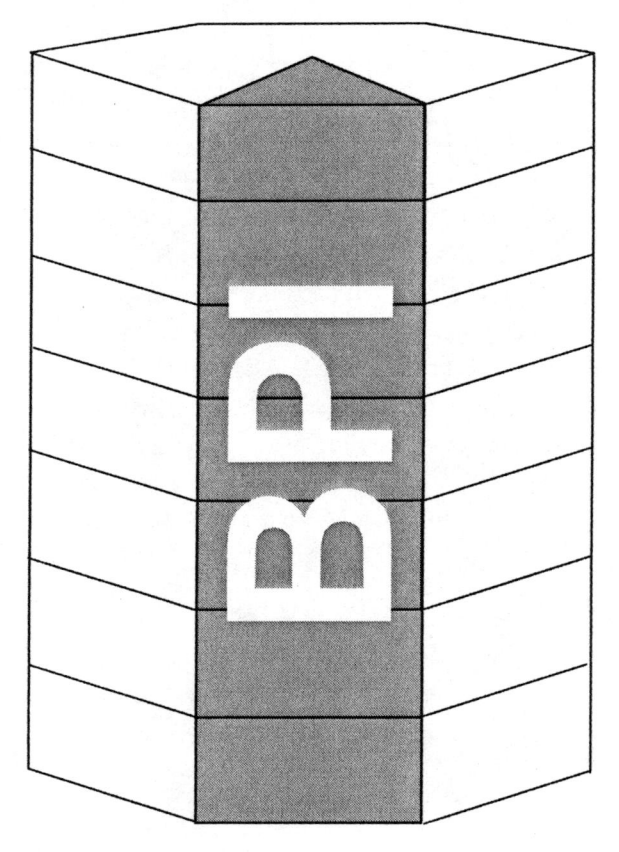

Ultimately, businesses should keep in mind that BPI is an ideal way to get a jumpstart on integration because it in no way limits future integration decisions. It is an affordable, all-purpose tool that can be used for the overwhelming majority of integration work. And, as we will see shortly, if a company later decides or discovers it needs an ETL tool or another specialized application, such as a document management system, it can use this tool in conjunction with BPI with excellent results.

# 4

# The Myths of Integration

## Early Myths

With every new technology comes a period of initial hype, followed by some disappointment as reality sets in. In the industry, this is often referred to as the "trough of disillusionment." But after a while, expectations become more reasonable, and the technology can be judged fairly on its own merit.

Without a doubt the hype of early marketing campaigns caused some setbacks for the integration industry. At first the prevailing tendency was to grossly understate the difficulty of providing and implementing integration solutions. After all, what vendor would publish a glossy brochure titled, "Integration Technology: The Five-Hundred-Step Guide to Building Your Own Phone Company"? In part as a result of early marketing promises, as well as the variety of new technologies and standards being introduced at the time, a number of myths began to circulate that were widely accepted as fact.

- *Myth #1: Companies can solve integration problems by moving everything onto a single system, such as SAP or PeopleSoft.* Few if any companies today can afford the luxury of tearing out all their systems and replacing them with a cohesive application that supposedly will run the entire business. In addition, no single application can offer best-of-breed functionality across the board. The package may have strong capabilities in human resources management, for example, but its inventory capabilities may fall short when compared to software applications that were developed exclusively for that purpose. Even if a company were to consider this type of massive undertaking, it would have to answer many tough questions. How long will this project take? Will business requirements have changed by the time the job is done, or will new requirements be introduced? What will happen in the event of a merger or an acquisition? And what about external partners, whose applications cannot possibly be moved onto the new, giant system that will supposedly solve every integration problem? To stay viable, companies have to deal with new systems and add-ons, as well as the retiring of outdated systems. Business process integration accepts the diversity and disparateness of applications and processes without requiring replacement or overhaul of existing systems.

- *Myth #2: Companies can buy infrastructure.* The idea that companies can "purchase" infrastructure and immediately begin implementing integration projects is far from the truth. Tools can be acquired, but infrastructure must be *built*. Businesses can purchase application servers, middleware, or tools that allow data transformation, but there is nothing "automatic" about these acquisitions that allows organizations to magically hurdle integration obstacles. In short, companies can acquire building blocks that provide the wherewithal to develop integration solutions, but significant technical expertise is still required. For example, application server technologies provide an excellent foundation for achieving load balancing, fault tolerance, and failover, but require a substantial amount of expert programming, particularly in the face of heterogeneous component models and types.

- *Myth #3: Building components gets companies integrated.* Perhaps the most notable misconception was that companies could achieve integration through componentization, using popular technologies like EJBs (Enterprise JavaBeans), COM (Microsoft's Component Object Model, now referred to as COM+), or CORBA (Common Object Request Broker Architecture). While it is possible for components to function in a standalone manner, they typically provide only part of the functionality required for a successful integration solution. Creating components is merely a beginning. Application server products provide an infrastructure or container for the execution and management of software components, but what is missing from the equation is the business logic that ties the components together to create a business process. This requires organizations to write a significant amount of sophisticated code, often in Java, that is time-consuming and often a major challenge when there are not enough developers with the necessary expertise.

- *Myth #4: Organizations tend to standardize on a single component model.* Despite a company's best intentions to standardize on a single component model, technology decisions are often made independently within departments or divisions. Further, no organization is immune to merger and acquisition activity, which may unexpectedly introduce non-standard systems. Finally, legacy systems always will be a factor. It is unrealistic to expect organizations to rewrite components using a different model every few years, and eventually the disparate component models and legacy systems must be tied together. Clearly, there are many benefits to componentization, but components alone do not allow a company to achieve integration. The market wants a solution to the difficult task of implementing the infrastructure required to build and deploy distributed, component-based solutions for e-business.

- *Myth #5: Once a company has integrated its data, everything falls into place.* When a company uses ETL tools that facilitate the moving of data from one system to another system that requires the data in a different format, one could argue that the company's systems are connected and can communicate freely with each other. However, much like componentization efforts, this represents only one step toward achieving true business integration. It does not address integration with business partners outside the firewall, for example. Perhaps more importantly, ETL tools alone do not give companies the capability to develop the new business processes that will take advantage of the integrated data. Data alone may produce useful reports, but without business logic, it will not serve the company's business needs.

## Recent Myths

The myths we've discussed thus far came about in the early days of integration technology, but recent developments have added some new misconceptions to the fray.

- *Myth #6: Web services eliminates the need for integration.* It's safe to say that Web services will play a critical role in future integration projects and, as with any other component technology, will go a long way to promote reusability. However, some of the initial hype has given way to the reality that Web services will never completely eliminate the need for integration. Web services can wrap separate pieces of functionality and expose these. But Web services does not address the tying together of these discrete functions. Even if every application is Web-service enabled, the company still must find a way to automate processes that include business logic and interact with multiple applications. Another problem with the Web services theory is the assumption – or requirement – that everything be Web-service enabled. Retrofitting every application with Web services interfaces would be more time-consuming and expensive than most companies can afford. It is also unlikely that every new application will routinely include Web services interfaces, especially in smaller companies that do not have extensive expertise in this area. In addition, current Web services tools and platforms are immature and do not address the daunting task of integrating XML-based interfaces. Writing Java code to integrate components on an application server is challenging enough, but writing Java code to integrate XML documents is infinitely more problematic.

- *Myth #7: Integration is prohibitively expensive and can't be done quickly.* The most prevalent myth today represents a complete reversal of the thinking in the earliest days of integration. Instead of the Pollyanna views that componentization or data integration makes business integration a snap, the industry now must combat the sentiment, especially among mid-market companies, that "integration is not for us." And while it may be true that *traditional* approaches to integration aren't suitable for mid-market companies because they are too expensive and slow-moving, BPI is putting the benefits of integration within reach of every company.

# 5

# The Top-down Approach to Integration

## Richard Schultz

### Seeing Is Believing

Programming tends to be more of an art than a science, and every developer has a unique style. There may be any number of ways to code the same business logic, with different groups using different approaches. This is one of the reasons custom code can be so difficult to analyze and debug, especially when it is not properly documented and the original developer has moved on. When a company needs to modify this code to add or change business logic, and a new set of eyes is trying to sort through the code for the first time, the company's business agility is severely affected. There is a very high risk of introducing new bugs into the existing application, and rigorous regression testing is a must.

Most business analysts need some sort of visual representation of the processes they are charged with designing or altering. Some use flowcharts; others use Visio diagrams; and analysts frequently include these in the specifications from which the developer writes code. After the first design session, it is a relatively quick exercise to modify a flowchart to fine-tune the business process, but it is infinitely more time-consuming to modify custom code to do the same.

In many ways, the handing over of paper specifications and diagrams to a developer is similar to the type of manual process that BPI aims to eliminate. It is not too far off from employees re-keying information from one system into a second system because the two applications are not compatible. Just as integration technology eliminates rekeying by allowing data to flow between disparate systems, BPI uses *graphical process models* to eliminate the need for developers to translate a business analyst's processes into code. This is, without a doubt, one of the most important and unique features of BPI software, and it opens the door to what we refer to as a top-down approach to integration.

# Kiss the Frog

## I Work with Models

Graphical process models are similar to flowcharts and workflow diagrams in that they describe how the business process will work. (They should not be confused with graphical user interfaces, which are what a user sees when interacting with modern applications, such as those found on a company's Web site.) But unlike paper charts or static diagrams, they are created in the same software package that ultimately will be used to connect to the existing systems and databases. Eventually these models are translated into executable programs that customers, partners, and suppliers can access. To get a better understanding of graphical process modeling, let's take an example and walk through the first few steps involved in designing and testing a business process that interacts with multiple applications.

In our example, a business wants to automate some of the processes involved in underwriting life insurance applications. The current processes are manual and require a significant amount of rekeying because the various systems used in the process are built with different technologies.

- First, the company must enter the insurance application information into its underwriting system.
- The company then checks its contract and license system to verify that the selling agent is authorized to write business in the state where the policy will be issued.
- Next the company accesses the Medical Information Bureau service to determine whether other insurance companies have reported a medical condition that was not disclosed on the application.
- The company also interacts with a third-party system to view the results of the applicant's blood work.

Other steps and systems are involved, but these will suffice for our example. Naturally the business analyst needs to understand how the automated process will work; this is a prerequisite in any type of application development or integration work. However, it is not necessary for the businessperson to understand the *technical details* of the systems that will participate in the process; in fact, the analyst does not even need to know whether the systems are mainframes or Java- or COM-based applications.

BPI software includes a modeling environment, which is the canvas where the analyst draws the processes. The analyst begins by drawing in the canvas the "activities" that represent steps in the overall business process. Activities are simply placeholders with labels. As the illustration shows, the analyst has created activities for the following steps:

- Adding the policy information
- Verifying the agent's contract and license
- Checking for undisclosed medical conditions
- Obtaining the results of the applicant's blood work

## Graphical Process Model

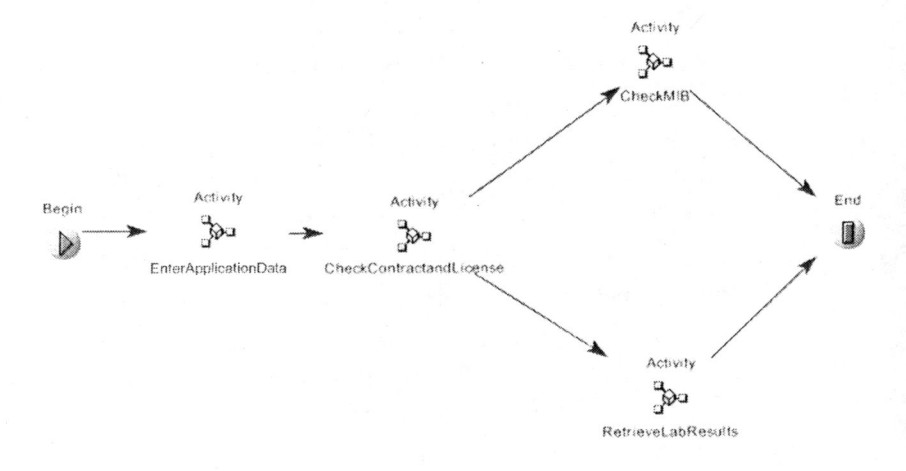

# Kiss the Frog

The business analyst also will describe the processing sequence, indicating the steps that must execute in a linear fashion and those that can execute concurrently. In this example, we quickly notice that the policy information is entered first; the agent's contract and license are verified next; and after these steps are successfully completed, the last two steps can occur simultaneously.

This is a very simple business process, but in the real world processes can be extremely complex, so BPI software equips business designers with an impressive arsenal of tools to create business rules. One particularly useful modeling construct is the ability to include conditional logic; that is, the analyst can define steps that execute only when a particular business rule applies. In our example, the analyst has constructed the process so that it will send a message to the agency if there is a problem with the contract or license. If there are no issues with the selling agent, this step will be ignored. All other steps will occur each time the process runs.

## Conditional Logic

Begin → Activity: EnterApplicationData → Activity: CheckContractandLicense → (AgentNotLicensed) → Activity: CheckMIB / Activity: NotifyAgency / Activity: RetrieveLabResults → End

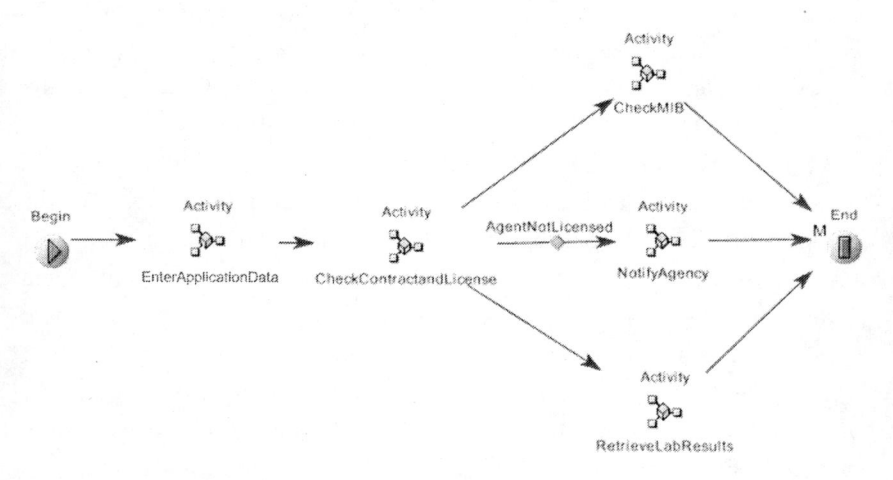

Using these intuitive tools, the business analyst can complete the first cut in a matter of minutes. At this point the graphical model will look the same, regardless of the type of technology with which the various systems were developed. From the businessperson's perspective, it does not matter at this point whether the external medical information is accessed as a Web service or via a mainframe.

## Tearing Down the IT Wall

If this business process were not designed using BPI software, the analyst would have to supplement the illustration with documentation and "throw it over the IT wall" to the development team, wait for the process to be coded (or worse, wait for an estimate indicating how long the coding would take), and hope for the best.

With BPI, instead of hoping the developers correctly interpret the business process illustration and associated documentation, the analyst brings the developers into the mix much earlier, and they work together for the remainder of the project. They will both use the model to continue the integration process. The developers do not have to worry about coding business rules because they are defined already. Instead, the developers concentrate on making the activities come to life by binding them to the systems that will execute the functionality.

In our example, as in most real-life scenarios, the new process will include steps that are carried out today by at least one system in the company's suite of applications. Every insurance company, large or small, has a system that retrieves agent information based on an agent code or social security number. Likewise, insurance carriers must be able to enter policy application information into an underwriting system.

Assuming the company uses the contract and licensing system to verify that the agent is authorized to sell the insurance policy, it is likely that users would enter the agent code or the social security number and see a screen that displays the pertinent information. This is the front-end view, but behind the scenes a method or function would take the agent code or social security number as an input and return the licensing details. While the front-end view is important to the analyst, what happens under the covers is much more important from the developer's perspective. A developer who was familiar with the contract and licensing system would use what the BPI industry refers to as a *connector* or *adaptor*, and bind (connect) the activity in the graphical process model to the piece of the application that provides the business functionality. These connectors require *no coding*; it is a simple matter of pointing-and-clicking through a few screens and browsing to the appropriate method or function.

This process would continue for each of the steps in the business process that are tied to a particular application or database. In all cases the developers are pointing-and-clicking as opposed to writing code, although the connectors may work slightly differently, depending on what technology is being accessed. If information must be retrieved from a database, developers can browse a set of stored procedures, for example. Soon the same graphical model the business analyst drew in the modeling environment is connected to each system that will perform its part in the overall business process.

## Speeding Development and Maximizing Skill Sets

Today companies feel the pressure to roll out solutions rapidly, and that means finding ways to slash what historically has been a lengthy and often inefficient development cycle. One of the biggest culprits has been miscommunication or back-and-forth wheel spinning caused by inadequate specifications, coupled with the development team's lack of business knowledge or the business side's inability to understand the technical nuances that affect the project.

Productivity with BPI increases for all involved. Everyone contributing to the project does what he or she is best at. Business analysts focus on business issues and business processes without being forced to make technical concessions up front, and developers can concentrate on connecting to existing functionality without learning every aspect of the business. Further, the developers work on the systems with which they are most familiar and where they add the most value.

Obviously, the point-and-click connectors present major timesaving opportunities. After all, why should the company in our example reinvent a way to look up licensing information when it already has a mechanism it uses in production every day? But the savings extend beyond not having to reproduce functionality. With no custom code to connect to back-end systems or data sources, companies avoid extensive regression testing, another major obstacle that stands in the way of making solutions available to customers and business partners.

A core value of BPI is its ability to leverage the mix of vision, thought processes, talent, and skills of technical and non-technical employees through one common solution. When the worlds of business and technology are closely aligned, business goals have a greater chance of being achieved through supporting technology. BPI provides the opportunity for businesspeople to have more control over how technology is used to meet business needs in an organization. BPI marries the business side and the technical side in a union that can only make the company stronger.

## Taking It from the Top

In the past when companies thought about integration, they invariably fixated on managing their data and figuring out a way to move it seamlessly from system to system. They knew different applications that required data in different formats were going to present difficulties. As we have seen in the case of the integration infrastructure stack, organizations essentially *began* their efforts by developing an architecture that supports the transfer and translation of their business *data*.

Solutions based on ETL tools and brokering messages tend to ignore the business processes until it is too late. When data drives the

## Kiss the Frog

business, it can force the business to function in a certain way and compromise the goals the company is trying to achieve. The data is required to support the business processes, but history shows that viewing the data and the processes as one and the same will result in failure of the company to see the real business issues. Instead, the company will see only what the data allows it to see. When business managers in the past were told by their IT counterparts, "That will take forever," or "There's no way to do that," chances are that this unwelcome news was based primarily on issues involving the business data.

The right BPI solution takes the focus off the data and puts it on the process, changing the company from a data-centric entity to a process-centric organization. Instead of tackling integration from the bottom up, companies should approach integration from the top down. In other words, the emphasis must be on the business problems the company is trying to solve. By first understanding and defining the processes they need, companies can then determine the best way to conduct business. Once the company defines the processes, using graphical modeling capabilities, it can easily leverage the data that supports the processes. This is in direct contrast to data-centric solutions that require building the process from the data up.

When businesspeople use BPI software to design processes, they do not have to be overly concerned with the particular technology of the systems involved. In the early stages of design they also do not have to worry about the exact data that will be moved between activities in the process or what format the data will need to be in en route to its final destination. The businesspeople can get a quick start on the most important aspect of the project – *how the automated process needs to function to increase efficiency and improve customer satisfaction.*

As the development phase progresses and when it is time to connect the steps in the process to the systems required to carry out each step, the implementers can still keep the big picture in perspective, as opposed to prematurely drilling down into the data weeds. Of course, to satisfy the business functionality, the developers will have to give consideration to the data inputs required and outputs returned in each step. (In our example the agent code or social security number was the input, and the output was the licensing information, which could be made up of several individual pieces of data.) However, moving the data and reformatting it along the way have been relegated to implementation details instead of the starting point for the entire project.

**BPI Data Mapping**

The reprioritization and reordering of the phases of the development cycle do not trivialize the job of moving the data from system to system. In fact, in all likelihood it will still be one of the most time-consuming aspects of integration projects because data will be represented differently from system to system. However, it does put the task into proper perspective. More important is that it removes some of the burden from the development team because it allows the business analyst to contribute to the data mapping chores.

The main reason analysts can contribute to or even handle the bulk of the movement of data between applications is that BPI products have a visual interface to simplify the moving of data from one step to the next. The BPI software will show, graphically, the specific pieces of data that are required to kick off each step, as well as the outputs that will be returned when the step completes. Thanks to this graphical interface, developers and business analysts can point-and-click to draw lines and map the data from one system to the next – for example, they can indicate which pieces of data from the underwriting system need to be passed to the contracting and licensing system to retrieve the agent's information.

## Visual Data Mapping

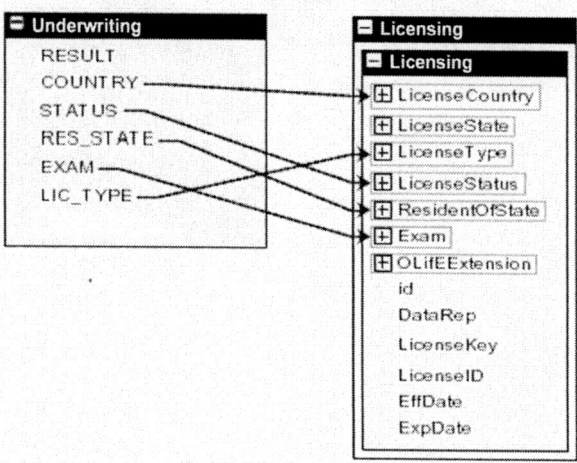

```
Underwriting                    Licensing
  RESULT                          Licensing
  COUNTRY                           ⊞ LicenseCountry
  STATUS                            ⊞ LicenseState
  RES_STATE                         ⊞ LicenseType
  EXAM                              ⊞ LicenseStatus
  LIC_TYPE                          ⊞ ResidentOfState
                                    ⊞ Exam
                                    ⊞ OLifEExtension
                                    id
                                    DataRep
                                    LicenseKey
                                    LicenseID
                                    EffDate
                                    ExpDate
```

BPI software also allows data transformation involving complex data structures. For instance, something as simple as an address can be made up of any number of data elements (apartment number, street, city, zip code, and so on). Complicating matters further, one system might include Address Line 2 and Address Line 3 fields; whereas, another system might not. The seemingly simple task of mapping one address to another can actually be quite tricky, so the ability to do this visually is very important. Business processes can also require special manipulation of data, such as joining two separate fields called "first name" and "last name" to make one new "customer name" field, for example, or applying rules to massage data into the format required by a particular system. Analysts can also use BPI to create a brand new representation of the data that may meet business needs not anticipated when a particular system was developed. Further, BPI offers a comprehensive set of functions that supplement the business logic between steps in the graphical process models. For instance, the analyst might include logic in one particular step that checks the agent's current status and creates a report listing all agents whose licenses have been temporarily suspended.

63

The bottom line is that BPI's graphical approach to data mapping gives analysts the tools to manipulate and transform data as the process dictates, without requiring programming expertise. No longer do the businesspeople have to sit back helplessly while they wait for the development team to do the heavy lifting; they can roll up their sleeves and contribute to integration projects in ways that were never possible before.

# 6

# The Continuously Evolving Business

**Richard Schultz**

## Evolution versus Transition

In the early days of integration, employees frequently equated large integration projects with impending job loss. These fears were not unfounded. In conjunction with these projects, companies frequently brought in the dreaded "change consultants" or set up "transition centers" to assist employees with resume writing or job hunting because their positions were being eliminated because of the retirement of a particular system or technology.

This notion of *transition* implied a finish, or a completed process. The idea was that after the integration project, companies would have successfully migrated from Point A to Point B, with Point B being a place where the organization could put aside its integration worries and return to business as usual.

Most businesses now realize there is no such thing as a predictable business-as-usual state that will carry them into the next few years or even the next few months. If anything, business as usual means companies will be faced constantly with new and changing requirements. For this reason the idea of transition has given way to the concept of *evolution*, which connotes ongoing change and growth. What is needed is a mechanism to manage this ongoing change and growth by giving companies more flexibility and agility than ever before.

A company's continuous evolution does not have to be as painful as the transitions of the past. This is not to say that BPI and downsizing are mutually exclusive, but rather that integration is now accepted, for the most part, as a business imperative. The only questions are when and how each business will choose to integrate. Customers expect and demand product variety and service delivery that can be achieved only through integration. Companies can seize opportunities to automate manual processes and free employees to work on activities where human intervention and judgment add value to customers or where the employees' particular talents will make the greatest impact. As a result, employees at all levels can be less apprehensive about integration and realize it is a key to their companies' success. With the right approach to integration, developers do not have to feel threatened by an army of consultants who are proficient in new technologies, and as we saw in the last chapter, business analysts may welcome the opportunity to contribute in exciting new ways to important integration projects.

## Indecision is the Key to Flexibility

In the past when companies made major decisions regarding their infrastructure, the decision makers may have consciously or subconsciously locked the company onto a path that took it years into the future. For example, companies committed to mainframe architecture designed and constructed entire buildings to secure the mainframe, wrote all their applications for the mainframe, hired developers who knew COBOL, Fortran, or other mainframe languages, and so on. Likewise, a few years ago, when companies first headed down the road to componentization, they invested heavily in application servers and launched hiring campaigns to bring on board developers who were familiar with CORBA, COM, or EJBs.

There was nothing wrong with these technology decisions; in fact, early adopters of mainframe technology no doubt enjoyed countless competitive advantages. The problem came when companies needed to evolve to accommodate new technologies and reap the benefits that came with these innovations. In the case of the integration infrastructure stack, it was extraordinarily difficult to bring new technologies into the mix.

Companies ideally want an integration solution that does not bolt to the floor, or even to a particular set of standards. Standards are important and extraordinarily useful in any corporation, but there is no guarantee that today's standards will hold up five years from now. In the music industry, vinyl LPs were the standard for years, but today they are essentially collectors' items, and it is no easy task to find a store that will replace the cartridge on a twenty-five year old turntable. From the record company's perspective, a successful company was one that could not only comply with the 33-1/3 and 45 RPM industry standards at the time, but also make the eventual transition to the compact disc format that has become the standard of today. A music fan today who wishes to buy a new stereo system will be better off buying a packaged system that includes a separate receiver, tape deck, and CD player, as opposed to a single system that includes these components. If CDs, as signs indicate, go the way of record albums in favor of a new technology, the consumer will be insulated from this shift in standards.

The company's decision makers want to keep the company evolving and flexible at the same time. BPI represents the first opportunity in the history of information technology for executive decision makers to say, "We're going to implement a solution that gives us the flexibility to use whatever new systems we choose, along with those we already have." A company doesn't have to get off the mainframe or adopt Web services before it is ready; with BPI, these technologies can co-exist peacefully and symbiotically.

Decision makers want to be freed from making a huge commitment around which so many other commitments must be made. C-level executives don't want to risk their careers or their company's wellbeing on the viability or longevity of a single standard or technology. They want room for indecision, which, as they say, is the key to flexibility.

### Creating an Effective Workforce

We've seen how the lack of specialized staff can contribute to a company's integration woes by forcing it to rely heavily on consultants or hire new, unproven developers whose resumes list experience with the company's newly adopted standards or technologies. In addition to burdening organizations with consulting bills or additional salary expenses, a traditional approach to integration might force a company to water down its workforce by letting go of extraordinarily good Visual Basic or mainframe developers and replacing them with average or below-average programmers who can write EJBs or COM objects.

## Kiss the Frog

Companies standardizing on a particular technology might also consider a major retraining initiative, but this too can be prohibitively expensive and will not instantly result in an expert staff to tackle new projects. Adding to the cost of these training efforts is the fact that they almost always must be conducted offsite. After all, if the business had the staff, curriculum, and materials to teach a particular technology discipline, chances are there already would be a significant amount of in-house expertise, and therefore the company would not need the training in the first place.

Few organizations are fortunate enough to have an all-star cast of developers who can work effectively with several different technologies. Ideally, companies want their developers deployed on projects where they will be able to use their expertise to make the greatest possible impact – for example by improving application functionality or working on features that customers actually see. BPI requires employees to learn the BPI software, which, because of its graphical nature takes only a few days, but it does not force a COBOL developer to learn Java or vice versa. In fact, if a company is going to integrate COBOL- and Java-based applications, each developer will be instrumental in identifying the programs and methods that execute the desired functionality. As we saw in the preceding chapter, the developer will play a crucial role in handling the technical connectivity details. Even when the newly automated business processes require functionality that does not exist in any one system, the company can have its experienced developers write the new business logic in the language they know best. Once the new functionality is incorporated into an existing system or as a standalone component, the company can use BPI to connect to it and incorporate it into new business processes.

By contrast, when companies tackle integration using a point-to-point approach, they seldom tap the full potential of their developers. In fact, much of the custom coding for these projects is a tedious and time-consuming low-level development effort that adds no business value whatsoever. Companies also have fewer options when they need to introduce business logic that currently is not performed by any of their existing systems. Whereas with BPI the company has the flexibility to write the new logic in any number of technologies or use the graphical modeling environment to introduce the new business rules, the company without BPI has limited options. Since point-to-point solutions generally require the business logic to be executed on an application server, the company may have an entire crew of developers who are not versed in this technology and will have difficulty playing a major part in the integration project.

It is best for companies to make their business analysts equal partners in integration projects. Companies have seen traditional integration projects falter because of the businessperson's inability to play a lead role in major development efforts – including the development of project estimates or even the feasibility of the initiative in general. In the past, if the IT team determined that a particular aspect of an integration effort would take months to build, there was very little assistance the business experts could offer.

For the true business expert who knows the capabilities of the various systems in the company's arsenal, BPI removes a great deal of uncertainty and allows the expert to flourish. If the project goal is to combine functionality that already exists but is spread across multiple systems, there is no question about the project's viability. The business expert already knows the functionality works and which applications do the heavy lifting. More important is that the businessperson can take charge and orchestrate the business processes, freeing the developer to concentrate on accessing the existing APIs (application programming interfaces) and handling the technical details.

In short, BPI tools have made it possible for business analysts to undertake many integration functions formerly handled by programming specialists, empowering these individuals and transforming the organization from an application-centric to a business process-centric entity.

## Kiss the Frog

## Web Today, Web Services Tomorrow

We have heard much about the opportunities the Internet has created and how it has changed the business landscape forever, but by no means does a company want to be required to expose every business process on its Web site. BPI gives a company great flexibility because it does not limit the company to a single front end; the same business process can be made available to different users in any number of ways. For that matter, a business process does not even have to have a user interface – for example, an internal process that runs on a predetermined schedule or as the result of a particular event.

The ability to create multiple interfaces for the same process allows businesses to integrate new processes with existing batch processes, Java applications, portals, and so on. Since most business processes will be the same no matter which customers and partners invoke them, the company has the flexibility to make the processes available to anyone with whom it wishes to do business. Organizations also gain the freedom to change direction at any time, so companies that drive transactions through their Web sites today can make the same transactions available as Web services tomorrow.

This front-end flexibility also allows companies to preserve their investments in front-end presentation technology. A company that has built a portal based on ColdFusion can easily integrate business processes that deliver data to the portal or respond to requests without having to switch to another presentation technology, like JavaServer Pages. The company surely will have significant ColdFusion expertise; it would make little sense not to leverage it. In a business climate where employees are expected to do more, common sense tells us it can only help if people are doing what they are good at in the first place.

## Building Key Partnerships

The ability to expose the same process as a Web service or via the company portal has a direct effect on a company's ability to grow its business through key partnerships. When companies make it easy to do business with other organizations that use different standards and technologies, they open the exchange of data to an unlimited number of players.

It is well known that a company's chances of attracting business partners decrease when it limits interaction to a particular type of transaction. This problem has been particularly apparent in the insurance industry, where a nationwide initiative known as SEMCI (Single Entry Multiple Company Interface) has been spurred by independent agents who have grown tired of logging on to the various Web sites of insurance companies to submit quote requests. Without SEMCI, if agents want to submit a quote to three companies, they must log on to three different Web sites and repeat the same process with three different user interfaces. In the following case study, we will see how one insurance company used BPI to improve the partnerships it had with its independent agents.

## Case Study: Improving Partner Relationships

*Integrating the systems of insurance companies with those of independent insurance agencies has been a pervasive problem for so long that a non-profit organization known as ACORD was formed in the 1970s to develop, maintain, and implement standards to promote the sharing of data among carriers, agencies, and third-party vendors. One of the most important standards in use today is ACORD XML, an offshoot of XML developed exclusively for the insurance industry that provides a generic way to represent and process data over the Internet.*

*The Mid-Market Insurance Company (MMIC) wanted to provide greater agent satisfaction by offering better service* and, in particular, faster turnaround times for insurance quotes and policy issuance.

The company had thus far been unable to take advantage of the ACORD XML standard, and its processes were slow and manually intensive. For example, when agents submitted applications to the company's underwriters, they had to mail or fax the paperwork to MMIC, even though they already had entered the application data into their agency management systems. MMIC would then have to re-key the same information into its policy administration systems. Further slowing the underwriting process was the need for motor vehicle reports, claim history reports, and other paperwork — none of which was available electronically because of system incompatibilities with the third-party vendors who provided the reports.

Providing insurance quotes, despite involving much less paperwork, was also extremely inefficient and a source of great agency frustration. Independent agents met with prospects, wrote down information, printed a quote request, and faxed the quote to MMIC. At MMIC, a data entry clerk entered the request into the AS/400 policy administration system, obtained the quote, and called the agency with the quote or faxed it back — sometimes as much as two days after receiving the original request.

Meanwhile, competitors who were ahead in the integration game had the ability to receive and respond to agency quote requests in real time. MMIC needed to compete, but it did not have a large IT staff and lacked the resources to build a complex integration infrastructure. In addition, MMIC's primary policy administration system was a legacy COBOL system running on an AS/400; it could not easily be modified or extended to receive ACORD XML data.

With the help of an intermediary that translates data from various agency management systems to ACORD XML, MMIC was able to accept incoming data from multiple agencies in a single, uniform format. Using BPI, MMIC designed and *implemented business processes that took this ACORD XML data and passed it to the policy administration systems needed to provide insurance quotes and generate policies for the applicants who met MMIC's underwriting guidelines.*

## Carrier Integration Solutions

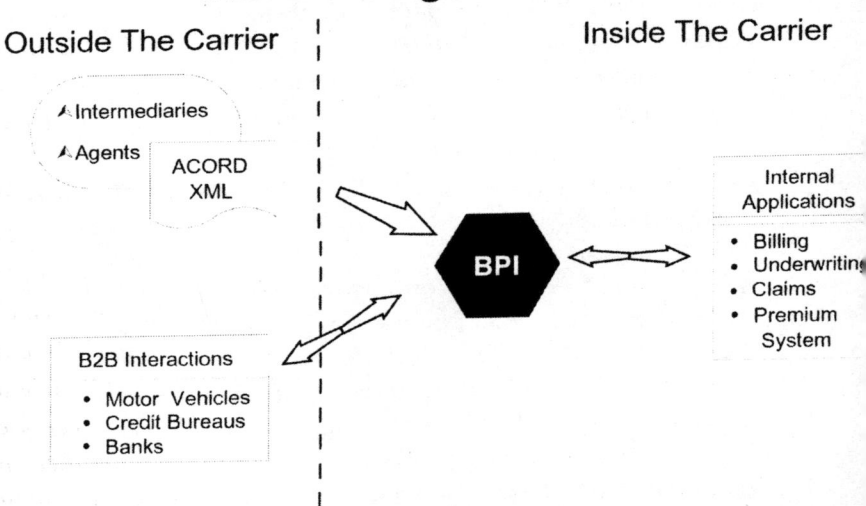

Outside The Carrier | Inside The Carrier

- Intermediaries
- Agents

ACORD XML

BPI

Internal Applications
- Billing
- Underwriting
- Claims
- Premium System

B2B Interactions
- Motor Vehicles
- Credit Bureaus
- Banks

*In just over three months, MMIC was able to respond to agency quote requests for its property and casualty business in real time and drastically reduce its underwriting cycle. In addition, MMIC's staff no longer has to re-key application data. This was accomplished without modifying the MMIC policy administration systems, which continued to provide useful functionality. And this was only the first step; MMIC is now poised to further streamline its underwriting process by accepting the third-party reports electronically. It is also rolling out the same type of solution for its commercial lines of business.*

# Kiss the Frog

## Redefining Relationships

Companies are striving not to impose particular data formats or technology standards on existing and potential business partners. All things being equal, if a partner has the option of working with two companies, and Company A requires the partner to convert business data into a specified format and Company B does not, Company B will be the overwhelming favorite for the partner's business. In fact, some businesses have begun to use BPI to build sophisticated "information gateways" that convert incoming and outbound data into whatever format a particular business partner requires.

BPI also can introduce new capabilities that radically redefine the relationships between existing business partners. Consider the notion of JIT (just-in-time) inventory, which will be familiar to anyone in the manufacturing sector. Perhaps a manufacturing company with a significant volume of purchasing transactions wants to reduce the costs and human labor associated with managing the inventory and making repeated calls to the vendor when each item needs to be replenished. With BPI, the customer can allow the vendor to access the inventory system, which would disclose not only current inventory levels, but also economic order quantities (EOQs) and the minimum daily or weekly inventory levels required for each item. Using BPI security features, the company could limit access to only the information needed by the vendor to manage inventory, and thereby protect key company information. By delegating to the vendor this responsibility, which would otherwise have been done in-house, the company would be able to reduce costs and increase efficiencies.

While the JIT concept already has benefited companies greatly, we can see that it may not yet have been stretched to its full potential. BPI can expand upon JIT capabilities by transferring the costs of managing inventories to the large vendors that supply materials. This is yet another example of how BPI can help a company reengineer its business in ways never before possible.

# 7

# The Bottom Line: Return On Investment

**Richard Schultz**

## ROI: The Buzz-phrase of the 2000s

Long gone are the days when companies purchased technology because it was considered state-of-the-art or for fear that they would fall behind competitors who had better, more sophisticated hardware and software. Several years ago, corporations had well staffed Research & Development departments, and the so-called tech-heads were encouraged to spend the better part of a day "playing" with and evaluating the latest technologies. Organizations looking for a reminder of these free-spending days need only look to the large collection of shelf-ware they have accumulated over the past two decades.

Today, no matter how great the potential of technology to solve business problems and enable companies to respond rapidly to changing market conditions, the company's decision makers will not pull the tech investment trigger without looking at the spending decision from a dollars-and-cents perspective. Return on Investment (ROI) is the buzz-phrase of the 2000s. Interestingly, as the phrase suggests, companies no longer think of paying for technology as just "spending" and now consider it "investing." To justify any major IT acquisition, organizations must be able to convince their budget keepers that any new hardware, software, or project will affect the bottom line positively – and quickly. If a company cannot make a case for ROI in twelve months or fewer, the chances of getting approval for the expenditure are greatly reduced.

In the 1990s, when companies launched large projects to build their integration infrastructure stacks, the timeframe was negotiable. Profits were up, and there was no particular urgency to demonstrate quick ROI, as long as the organization felt it was moving in the right direction and positioning itself for the future.

Now the timeframe is everything. Proposals for two-year initiatives can be dismissed out of hand, even before the PowerPoint presentation is finished, unless the project can provide ROI in two- or three- month increments along the way. Even customer service improvements and usability enhancements can be tough to push through, if the company

## Kiss the Frog

does not feel the improved service or user experience alone will generate significant additional revenue opportunities.

With the increased emphasis on shortened timeframes, companies are trying to avoid huge initial expenditures because these decrease the potential to achieve rapid ROI. The introduction of a productized or packaged integration solution in the form of BPI software could not come at a better time. Assuming companies have projects with the potential to increase revenue or cut operating costs, the cost of BPI greatly improves the possibility of demonstrating a rapid ROI.

### Danger in Numbers

Unfortunately, the intense focus on ROI brings with it the potential to make ill-advised decisions. There is a very real danger that companies may take the ROI calculations too literally and force themselves to assign somewhat arbitrary dollar values to costs and benefits that are virtually impossible to quantify.

Companies can get a reasonable handle on benefits like increased revenues, reduced maintenance costs, or savings in human labor, but how do they measure the dollar value of a project that will result in improved customer satisfaction, for example? They hope this type of benefit will result in increased revenue, but it is impossible to forecast the specific dollar amount with certainty. Likewise, it is hard to come up with exact figures for projects that result in the ability to bring products to market more quickly or initiatives that open new revenue channels, like e-commerce with partners and self-service portals. Most of these benefits will have *some* type of a ripple effect – but how much? The same is true for projects that will reduce processing errors by eliminating manual entry. It's very possible, for instance, that these types of undertakings could affect the number of goods that are shipped to customers in error. While this type of analysis and extrapolation is definitely a worthwhile exercise, a company will be hard pressed to turn it into an exact dollar amount.

Based on experience, companies also are taking great pains to factor in potential indirect costs that could drive up the total cost of ownership (TCO), thereby lowering the ROI. When it comes to sophisticated technology, the cost of the software license is seldom if ever the actual amount the company will spend to get the software running. Many of the indirect costs associated with integration historically have been hidden in the service-to-license ratio, which is the ratio of the cost of the services provided by the vendor to the cost of the technology itself.

The vendors who started marketing integration solutions years ago tended to have huge service-to-license ratios, often in the area of ten-to-one. If the company paid $400,000 for the technology that made up its integration infrastructure, it spent more than $4 million in services trying to put the pieces of the infrastructure together in a cohesive fashion. Integration vendors made the bulk of their money on these service dollars, and the longer the implementation cycle, the higher their profit margins. The software and tools were new; customers had virtually no chance of taking full advantage of them without onsite assistance. Naturally vendors did not market their products and services in this way; the vendors simply assured their customers they would provide whatever assistance might be needed to get the new system up and running. As the vendors worked with their customers through the learning curve to full implementation, the vendors submitted periodic bills for the services they were providing. As long as some form of progress was being made, it was much easier for customers to concentrate on potential benefits than to worry about service costs, especially when vendors were, in most instances, genuinely attempting to provide quality customer service. Even when progress wasn't so obvious, companies had little alternative but to keep things moving and put their faith in the expertise of the integration vendors. Meanwhile the service costs kept building, month by month, until the cost of the project ended up in the millions.

Because of this, many businesses feel they've been held hostage in the past by integration vendors and are extraordinarily cautious about signing any type of contract without an in-depth analysis of potential service fees and their impact on TCO. This is another factor that has helped opened the door for an approach to integration that is easier to learn – a solution that customers can actually figure out on their own, with minimal training and onsite supervision.

## Non-invasive Technology

Service fees are just one example of indirect costs that can negatively affect a company's ROI and TCO. Other potential expenses include training costs, labor costs associated with writing custom code, ongoing maintenance requirements or regression testing, and the purchase of additional hardware or software – often unanticipated – that will be needed to make the integration project a success.

Companies seek to control many of these indirect costs by finding an integration solution that is *non-invasive*. In other words, companies want an approach that does not require them to modify existing systems. Most of their packaged applications, databases, and legacy mainframe systems are good at what they do. For example, in the case of custom-developed business applications, a significant amount of expertise went into their construction, and countless business rules are embedded into these systems. There is no reason these systems cannot or should not be used as they are.

This non-invasive approach can extend beyond a company's business applications and apply to the infrastructure stack. Companies that use application servers or messaging middleware do so because these technologies provide useful functionality. This is why the BPI graphical modeling environment and framework are designed to sit on top of the company's existing technology stack, rather than replace all or a portion of the stack. Companies that rely heavily on application servers can connect to the components being executed on them, which is conceptually the same as connecting to a particular piece of functionality handled by a mainframe or Visual Basic application.

A non-invasive approach to integration allows organizations to preserve and leverage their existing IT investments. By taking advantage of codeless connectors to access functionality that already works, companies can control costs by avoiding custom code, unnecessary complexity, ongoing maintenance burdens, and extensive regression testing.

## Demonstrating Incremental Results

On the benefits side of the ROI equation, companies are looking for quick hits – projects they can roll out quickly as evidence that their technology solution supports key business goals. In addition, companies realize that cash inflows that will not be realized for a year or more must be discounted because the value of a dollar today is worth far more than a dollar will be worth twelve months from now.

Many companies have found it makes sense to tackle small projects that tie together functionality from two or three applications before taking on larger projects that require more upfront analysis and involve many more systems. If a manufacturing firm wants to automate a complicated set of business processes that involve interaction with four separate applications that handle order entry, pricing, inventory, and order tracking, the firm can do so piecemeal, perhaps by starting with the pieces of the process that will produce the quickest ROI. BPI does not require the company to integrate all four systems at once, or begin developing a point-to-point solution between two of the applications while hoping that, when the third and fourth systems are added to the recipe, the first point-to-point solution does not have to be completely revisited. Because the company can make progress without having to tinker with existing systems or write custom code, it can make these types of quick ROI hits without worrying about what will happen as soon as it tries to fold in functionality from the additional systems.

In the financial services sector, to meet the changing needs of their customers, companies roll out new products and services constantly – for example, new annuity products and innovative investment strategies. Quite often, these new offerings actually come together through a recombination of components from other products and services the company already provides. The company's decision-makers already know the ins and outs of annuities and how to formulate investment strategies. They can tweak these existing items to accommodate new rates or offer some other new attention-grabber, so the new product or service does not have to be entirely rewritten.

Companies want integration solutions that make a positive impact on product speed to market. They want a much more rapid cycle of evolution and maintenance, as well as the cost reductions that come from this accelerated cycle. Companies also are interested in features specifically designed to promote reusability, so it is worth emphasizing that *any graphical model drawn in a BPI modeling environment can be used in its entirety as part of a larger, more complex process.* Depending on the particular BPI software, the business analyst can accomplish this as easily as dropping and dragging one existing graphical model into another. In the same fashion, existing functionality from the mainframe or any other system can be incorporated in as many business processes as desired, and all application and database connections can be reused. Once a connection is created and connectivity established, developers have the ability to add an unlimited array of methods that take advantage of the same connection. As a result, when the company is ready to broaden the scope of its integration initiatives, it already has as a starting point fully functional processes and methods that have been tested in the production environment.

Incremental approaches also provide another advantage. Companies can temporarily ignore applications that do not directly contribute to the new business processes they are automating. This is in direct contrast to projects that require the company to tie everything together via a message bus before developing any new functionality. When BPI is in place, if a company's focus changes after the initial project, the company loses nothing. If tomorrow a new requirement comes along that necessitates the use of a system that was not needed initially, this change can be easily accommodated.

## Case Study: Incremental vs. Traditional Approach

*It's not often that a company gets two chances to tackle the same project. Last Chance Retirement Company (LCRC) purchased a contemporary packaged system to keep track of its agent licensing, contract, and commission information. The new system had the potential to provide a significant return on investment because its collection of existing systems was outdated and inefficient. The new system featured built-in edits and business rules that would help LCRC address complex business and regulatory requirements and eliminate a significant amount of manual entry, and LCRC was excited to roll it out.*

*Nearly two years later, the new system was not in production. There was nothing wrong with it, but LCRC had not counted on the complexities involved in integrating it with the rest of its business applications, which were built with a mix of technologies, including CICS, IMS, and DB2. The new system needed to feed and interface with many other applications for a variety of business functions, including compliance and reporting.*

*At first LCRC followed a traditional approach of writing customized COBOL programs that were designed to pass the new system's data to the company's other applications, but progress was slow. Expenses quickly mounted, and it became clear that the integration effort was growing unnecessarily complex. LCRC realized that, even if it could write all the necessary COBOL programs in record time, the resulting environment would be extremely difficult to maintain. More important, the company would be hard-pressed to accommodate new and changing business requirements.*

## Kiss the Frog

*Clearly, LCRC needed a better alternative. The company began to consider the benefits of modeling business processes graphically and connecting to existing functionality – without writing code. With little to lose after months of writing custom code, LCRC decided to try a low-risk BPI pilot that would allow it to use its new system while leaving intact the collection of old systems.*

*The pilot took just two weeks and was an unqualified success. Instead of writing COBOL programs, the pilot team modeled processes graphically and used point-and-click connectors to access the various applications. LCRC employees could now take advantage of the new system's contemporary interface – a huge timesaver – because the pilot team left the existing feeds from the collection of old systems in place and concentrated on making the new application interface with the systems it was designed to replace.*

*Because BPI allows an incremental approach, LCRC was able to meet its primary objectives of getting its new system in production and reaping the benefits of the new system's contemporary interface and built-in business rules. With the new system in place, LCRC is now free to work on follow-on projects and continue the pattern of demonstrating incremental results.*

BPI is changing the way business decision-makers think about integration by reducing the time and cost to implement, removing the custom-building factor, and eliminating the confusion associated with how business processes need to operate. A company's risk in terms of getting its systems up and running is greatly reduced. The company will know the cost of the BPI project ahead of time, and will thus have a far smaller likelihood of being blindsided by indirect costs that can arise during the implementation.

A significant but often ignored benefit of BPI is that as each new project is rolled out, the company's integration costs will shrink, since the software will already be in place, and the company and its staff will experience success early and often. The opposite is true for point-to-point solutions: They will not improve over time; maintenance and development costs will continue to increase; and each project will become progressively more difficult.

The illustration below compares BPI to point-to-point solutions.

## Rapid and Incremental Return With BPI

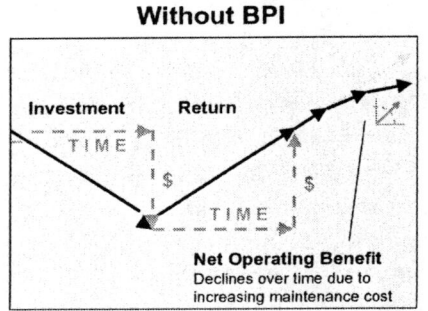

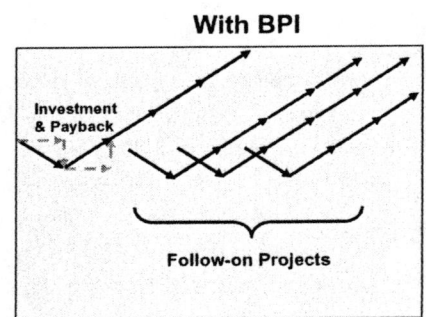

**Without BPI**

Investment   Return
TIME
$   $
TIME
**Net Operating Benefit**
Declines over time due to increasing maintenance cost

**With BPI**

Investment & Payback

**Follow-on Projects**

For a brief time in the life of the integration cycle, point-to-point solutions may be more cost-effective and easier to implement, but as time goes on, costs for point-to-point solutions spike dramatically as more effort and greater expertise become essential. With a productized approach to integration, however, costs decrease dramatically as the company takes the path toward scaling and profitability.

# 8

# Will the Real BPI Please Stand Up?

## The BPI Bandwagon

Because BPI has gained so much momentum and industry recognition, many vendors who formerly positioned themselves as providers of enterprise application integration technology now claim to support BPI or develop BPI software. This shift in marketing campaigns is not as abrupt as one might think; after all, BPI is intended to enable and solve the same problems that traditional approaches always have. It does, however, increase the importance of being able to easily distinguish software that provides the benefits of BPI from solutions that do not.

We have talked at length about what BPI solutions can accomplish at a high level, but let's take a closer look at some of the components that make up what the industry refers to as out-of-the-box BPI functionality. We'll also describe specific features of these components that can add to the software's overall desirability – features that companies should consider carefully when comparing the offerings of various BPI vendors.

# Automating Processes With BPI

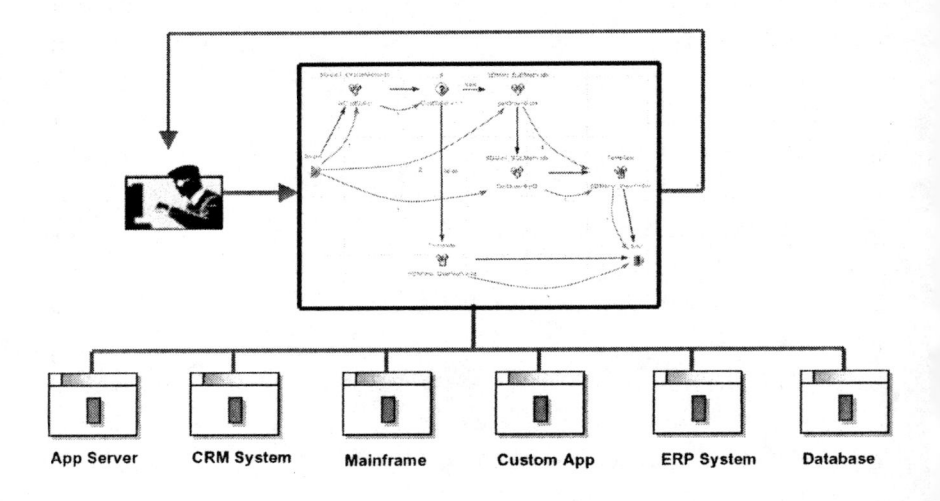

## The Graphical Modeling Environment

In Chapter 5 we discussed the benefits of a graphical modeling environment and touched on some of its capabilities. BPI software will vary substantially from vendor to vendor, but if the product doesn't have a graphical modeling environment, it is not BPI software.

The two most important aspects of the modeling environment are ease of use and the ability to represent complex, real-life processes. Businesspeople *must* be able to design processes easily; programming knowledge cannot be a prerequisite. Obviously, then, the businesspeople should be involved in the assessment of this part of the product, even if they do not participate in the entire evaluation process. Further, developers and non-developers alike must be able to view a graphical representation of a business process and make sense out of it. If the graphical models contain cryptic symbols or constructs that are difficult to learn or understand, the learning curve will go up, and the ability for the business and IT staff to collaborate on integration projects will be compromised.

At the same time, the modeling environment must allow analysts to represent the kinds of complex processes that exist in the real world. In Chapter 5 we described how a fairly simplistic business process might look in a graphical modeling environment. A better litmus test, however, is the way the modeling environment handles a complicated, multi-step process that requires the moving of data between various systems or the way it visually represents complicated business rules that affect the sequence of steps in a process or the systems with which the process interacts. Some modeling environments handle simple processes nicely, but quickly become cumbersome when the business processes increase in complexity. A business analyst evaluating a BPI product's modeling environment should not be afraid of asking the vendor to draw a particular graphical model based on a real-life business process with which the analyst is familiar.

As companies consider how they will use the modeling environment, some thought should be given to how well it supports the top-down approach to integration that is needed in today's business climate. In Chapter 5 we described an ideal scenario in which the business analyst first models the process without having to worry about the specific systems or technologies that will be involved. It is worth taking extra time to understand exactly how the graphical modeling environment will be used and, in particular, what percentage of the design work can be accomplished by business analysts before developers are required to assist with connectivity or complex data manipulation.

Process reusability is important, and companies should have a good understanding of how the graphical modeling environment supports the reuse of entire processes or certain steps in a particular process. For example, if a company plans to develop several solutions that will involve approving a customer's credit card payment, the company should have an idea of how it will reuse the credit card functionality after rolling out the first solution. Along these lines flexibility is also critical; businesspeople must be able to modify and fine-tune existing graphical models with minimal effort. But along with flexibility should come some sanity checks; the models should include edits that prevent analysts from creating invalid processes – that is, processes that cannot possibly execute at runtime because of logical errors or dependencies that have not been fully thought out.

The best graphical modeling environments are those that allow businesspeople to represent the widest variety of real-life processes, regardless of whether the processes are short- or long-running, are simple or complex, include steps that execute concurrently or execute based on certain conditions, require error handling, include human intervention, trigger external events or are triggered by them, and so on. For this reason, before evaluating the BPI software, companies should spend time thinking about some of their most complex business processes and use them as a mental backdrop as they scrutinize various BPI offerings.

## Kiss the Frog

## Data Mapping and Transformation

Data mapping and transformation capabilities are absolutely essential to BPI, but alone they do not constitute a BPI solution. A company should be wary of a vendor whose pitch focuses almost exclusively on what the solution can do with data; this may be a sign that the vendor is trying to put a BPI label on what is essentially a traditional approach to integration.

Why are the movement and transformation of data so critical? Typically each application or data source within a company provides different data or a slightly different representation of the same data; in fact, this is the root cause of many integration problems. To integrate the business functions of dissimilar systems, the person modeling business processes must be able to access different data and move it between applications, transforming the data into whatever format or representation a particular system or set of users requires.

We have pointed out that dealing with incompatible data is generally the most difficult and time-consuming aspect of integration projects; for this reason, a clean, easy-to-use interface for working with complex data is essential. As with the modeling environment, the company's businesspeople should be heavily involved in the evaluation of this aspect of the software and should feel confident that they will be able to assume many of the data-related responsibilities that traditionally have been relegated to developers.

Obviously, this means the data manipulation features must be graphical; business analysts should be able to map data from one system to another by drawing lines, pointing and clicking, or taking a comparably simple action. Any BPI product will be able to handle simple data mappings – for example, mapping the part number from the pricing system to the part number in the inventory application – but the distinction between competing BPI software packages will be how they handle complex data structures and complicated rules for transforming data.

91

Ideally, the BPI software's data manipulation capabilities will be tightly integrated with the graphical modeling environment, since most business processes are ultimately driven by business data. A product that deals with processes and data in relative isolation may not be as user-friendly as it first appears. It is difficult to get a solid handle on a process without knowing what data is involved; likewise, looking at data alone does not guarantee a good understanding of the process.

Some specific capabilities to consider include:

- *Built-in functions for transforming data, including string manipulation, math, and logic.* Companies must deal with an unlimited number of business rules that hinge specifically on business data. Many of these will be based on the specific *value* of a particular data element at runtime, and analysts need to be able to create business rules based on these values. Using a simple example, business analysts might need to apply pricing discounts if the customer orders more than ten items. (In the BPI software, this might require a function that examines the *value* of the *quantity* field.) Also many processes will execute differently, depending on the format, structure, or presence of particular data elements. For example, countless business processes include rules that govern whether the customer's business address, billing address, or shipping address should be used, depending on the particular transaction. String concatenation also is frequently required; business processes frequently result in new representations of data formed by combining one or more data elements from multiple systems.

- *Support for groups and lists of data, including the ability to examine specific items in the group or list.* For example, a manufacturing company might need to automate a business process that examines a list of items created in Shop A and a second list created in Shop B, and creates a new list that combines items based on common criteria

– perhaps all items shipped on a certain date or all goods ordered by a certain customer. The company might also need to calculate subtotals or the grand total of items retrieved from different sources, or to apply similar business rules that require sophisticated data mapping and transformation abilities.

- *The ability to aggregate data from multiple sources into a single target.* For example, in many organizations, customer information is scattered across the enterprise. This fragmentation of information typically occurs as a result of the implementation of discrete business systems over the years. The results are duplicate data and an inability to obtain a unified, 360° view of a customer. The data mapping features should allow business analysts to map the needed data elements from each system that contains valuable information into a single, standardized representation of a customer that meets the needs of the business process being modeled.

## Connectivity Framework

Broad connectivity is a requisite for BPI. Companies must be able to access data and functionality, regardless of where it resides or what kind of technology is involved. The BPI product itself must handle the connectivity, and this should be achieved without writing code. If the vendor insists on sending in a team of consultants to examine a company's systems or cannot arrange a simple onsite demonstration to connect to a live application or database, companies should proceed cautiously.

The BPI connectivity framework should not be biased toward any one technology or standard; business functionality on the mainframe is no more or less important than business functionality made accessible via a Web service. Companies looking at connector capabilities should therefore be diligent about examining how the product connects to different technologies. In its presentations or software demos, a particular vendor might showcase a specific connector that works particularly well for mainframe applications, but this does not necessarily mean every target application will be as easy to work with. An approach that relies on introspection of metadata (data about the data) from the target system or database to define how the system interaction will work is most advantageous. This eases the integration process by providing an easy way to view the inventory of specific interactions for each potential system that will take part in the automated processes.

## Metadata Introspection

- Agent_ID
  - getAgentInfo.sfmd
  - getAgentInfo
    - LIC_ID (Input/String)
    - RESULT (Output/String)
    - COUNTRY (Output/String)
    - STATUS (Output/String)
    - RES_STATE (Output/String)
    - EXAM (Output/String)
    - LIC_TYPE (Output/String)
    - LIC_STATUS (Output/String)

Ideally, the BPI connectors should provide the ability, without custom coding, to test existing functionality *before* it is included in a business process. This speeds the BPI development cycle dramatically. With a connector testing mechanism, users can provide the required inputs and view the outputs for a particular method or function in isolation. If business analysts know that the individual pieces of a process work before they merge them into a single process that may include a number of additional business rules, the company will save a significant amount of time trying to debug processes before they go into production.

## Runtime Engine

A company may be able to define extremely efficient, easy-to-understand business processes in the graphical modeling environment, but if the processes do not execute reliably in production, the company will have little to show for its integration efforts. The BPI product must include a robust and reliable runtime engine that manages the execution of processes and includes high-availability features. The engine must be designed to meet the requirements of straight-through processing in complex environments.

But as with the other BPI components, companies should be wary of vendors who place undue emphasis on the engine, processing power, messaging, or infrastructure in general. *Messaging capability by itself is not BPI.* Without question, the engine needs to provide a runtime environment to support the processes that are modeled graphically; but if the company must write code to handle business logic, it is not buying a BPI solution.

After data mapping and transformation work, companies undertaking integration projects probably spend the second-largest block of their time trying to configure their runtime environment so that it can handle large volumes of users in a 24 x 7 environment. Special attention should be paid to how the engine supports load balancing, fault tolerance, and scalability, which are essential when applications must be continuously available to a large population. Does the engine handle these features automatically, or does it merely *support* these features? If the solution requires supplementing the BPI engine with messaging servers or application servers to provide a truly reliable runtime environment, the company will need to examine these associated costs carefully and include them in its ROI calculations.

Security features merit careful scrutiny as well; in most cases, companies will want strict control over who can access the various business processes being implemented. Security issues inevitably will arise when dealing with confidential data or business partners outside the firewall, and it is a major timesaving feature when the engine's security mechanism can plug into security models that the company already has in place. The engine should conform to Java security standards, and it also should be able to integrate with LDAP (Lightweight Directory Access Protocol) directories, NT Domain, and other commonly used security frameworks for authenticating users and applying access control rules.

## BPI Components

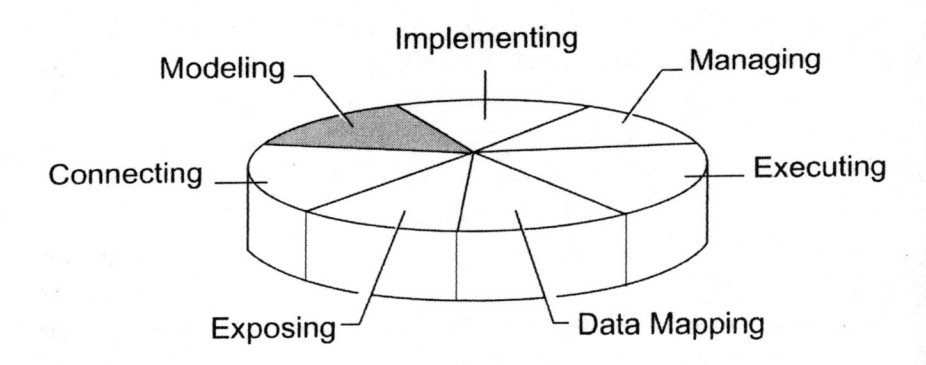

*Diagram: Pie chart showing BPI Components: Modeling, Implementing, Managing, Executing, Data Mapping, Exposing, Connecting*

### Management, Monitoring, and Debugging

BPI software must include some type of engine management console that allows administrators to control which processes are running in production and who has access to them. The management console also is typically used to configure session management features. A high-quality console should provide an easy-to-use graphical interface to simplify the administration of the runtime environment.

Along with the ability to manage processes, companies need a way to monitor what is happening at runtime. BAM (Business Activity Monitoring) is a hot buzz-phrase in the integration industry, even though most BPI products are relatively immature in this area. However, this

## Kiss the Frog

does not diminish its importance, especially for companies that have a high volume of activity or zero tolerance for processing errors. Depending on the business, companies will need to track the users who access the processes and the specific transactions that have occurred on various applications. If a particular process does not produce the expected result, companies need a fast, reliable way to dissect the steps that occurred during the process and isolate the piece of functionality that did not execute correctly. In a multi-step process that is passing and transforming a significant amount of data between applications, this can be a daunting task, so a good debugging mechanism is critical. Companies also will want to analyze runtime statistics to identify potential bottlenecks and improve throughput, since a large number of factors can govern the performance of any step or system.

### Exposing Processes: Integrating BPI into the Enterprise

When companies think about integration, they generally concentrate on the data and functionality that must be extracted from their incompatible back-end systems and spend less time thinking about the way they will actually invoke the automated processes. But once new processes are created, they must be incorporated into the business. This may include integration with existing business systems, new applications the company plans to roll out, Web sites, or partners' systems. Since the most common type of integration project involves making new functionality via a portal or company Web site, many companies do not consider the potential benefits of accessing business processes in multiple ways.

BPI should not be confused with ColdFusion, JavaServer Pages, or any other technology used primarily to develop application *front* ends. BPI is not about the beautification of a Web site or company portal, although it can certainly be used to gather the necessary data from multiple sources and organize it in a way that makes the presentation easier. The design or usability of a particular application does not necessarily require integration work; consequently, this type of front-end work is and should be beyond the scope of BPI software.

There is, however, a danger in dismissing front-end considerations completely. The same business process may need to be accessed from multiple systems, and each calling system will use a different technology. A good BPI solution should provide the ability to expose processes for maximum interaction; that is, anyone who needs to leverage the business processes should be able to access the process easily. A company that is planning integration solutions that will be accessed via avenues other than the Internet should examine the amount of work this will take and determine exactly how it will be accomplished. And even if the company has no immediate plans to expose processes with multiple interfaces, it is very likely that in the relatively near future, partners will want to access business processes as Web services. Companies need to be ready to address this demand.

## Implementation Methodology

Key to the success of any large development project, regardless of whether it requires integration technology, is a thoroughly considered, structured implementation methodology. When a company undertakes a BPI project, the specific methodology and requirements-gathering process can be quite different from what it is used to, although there are some similarities. Understanding the methodology recommended by BPI vendors can lend valuable insight into the product itself.

The most notable departures are the enforcement of the top-down approach to the project and business-IT collaboration that we have discussed throughout this book. This can be accomplished in a number of ways, but one popular approach is the adoption of a "living design document" that is the co-responsibility of the business staff *and* the IT people. The project leaders update this document at critical stages of the project, beginning with high-level descriptions of the business processes that will be automated. More importantly, the business analysts use the

## Kiss the Frog

graphical modeling environment to design these processes and include screen captures of the processes in the design document. In general, the ability earlier in the cycle to include more pictures in the design document – pictures that do not require translation – helps to keep projects moving rapidly.

The developers will add to the design document high-level information about the systems to which they are connecting, and include the specific methods, functions, and stored procedures they plan to use. Typically they will specify the expected inputs and outputs, as well. *This is done before any development actually begins.* As the project moves on, modifications will be made as necessary, and soon the document will be updated again with the data mapping and transformation specifics, including screenshots from the graphical interface used to manipulate the data.

The importance of the design document and this type of implementation approach cannot be overstated. The document records the work being done and helps generate buy-in *at all stages* of the project, from the businesspeople and the IT groups alike. This protects companies from going down blind alleys because a developer did not interpret a business analyst's specifications correctly or because of other types of project team miscommunication. All participants in the project contribute to the documentation, and everyone agrees on the final product. When it is finished, the company has a working specification document it can use the next time the application is modified or enhanced, complete with business process diagrams, details on the systems involved and the functionality provided by each, and the specific data elements used in the various processes.

## Workflow Capabilities

BPI should offer basic workflow features. Business analysts must be able to model processes that include human intervention, as well as straight-through processing. For example, the BPI software should allow analysts to model processes that pause while a decision is made or send an e-mail message indicating human intervention is required. If the analyst is modeling a billing process, and a supervisor's approval is required for payments that exceed a certain amount, the process should pause after being directed to someone who can authorize the payment. In addition, the process should follow two different paths after the decision, depending on whether the payment was approved or rejected.

As with other facets of integration work, there are times when a highly specialized workflow or document management system may be required for a particular project. Vendors who focus entirely on workflow or document management will offer an extensive set of capabilities, including roles or the ability to describe organizational structures. User interfaces can also be critical features, and, as we have mentioned, creating user interfaces is not one of the core capabilities of BPI.

A pharmaceutical company that must assemble and manage huge documents, such as those involved for new drug applications to the FDA, in all likelihood would need to supplement its BPI software with a best-of-breed document management system, but this by no means implies that the company could not use BPI for a large portion of its other integration work.

## Choosing the Right Product

No single BPI product is right for every company. Companies must make their decisions in the proper context – namely, by keeping in mind the specific integration baggage they carry and the types of solutions and partner relationships that are important to the company's success.

Competing software products in any market will have plusses and minuses, and BPI is no exception. For this reason companies must clearly understand their priorities. For example, do customers require a fully fault-tolerant, 24 x 7 environment? What kinds of audit trails are necessary for reporting, compliance, or problem resolution? How much

## Kiss the Frog

user volume does the company experience? Is transaction security or data confidentiality a key consideration? Do the processes need to be exposed from the Web site only?

These company-specific details are by far the most important criteria upon which the ultimate decision should be based. BPI software is still relatively new, and because of this it is unlikely that a single product will excel in all these areas. Those that have extremely good graphical modeling environments may require more work in the areas of connectivity or business activity monitoring; other products may have strong data mapping and transformation capabilities but may require more attention to high-availability features than others. It is especially important also that companies become familiar with the BPI vendor's roadmap — the types of features and functionality that are planned in subsequent product releases.

It is also essential to know what kinds of specific problems the vendor has solved in the past. If companies are struggling with HIPAA compliance or ACORD standards adoption, and a particular vendor has a long list of case studies in these areas, this experience is clearly of major importance.

The ultimate tiebreaker should be the BPI product's flexibility. No one can predict what the business landscape will be like five years from now, so companies should favor BPI vendors that do not appear to be betting on .NET or Java or Web services or something else to become the universal standard. The agile businesses are the ones that will survive, regardless of what unfolds next upon the IT stage.

# 9

# Preparing for the Future

**Richard Schultz**

## Acknowledge the Unknown; Work with the Known

Pick up a technology magazine, and chances are it will contain "The Future of Integration," or a similarly titled article. The article will talk about Web services, or perhaps about SOI (service-oriented integration), along with a comparison of .NET versus J2EE. Sprinkled in might be discussions about the maturation of UML (Universal Modeling Language), the evolution of standards, and any number of technology buzzwords that may or may not sound familiar. Each author's view of the future will be somewhat different, but most articles will share one commonality: They will offer little if any practical advice.

When we consider that the integration experts have been continuously defining and redefining EAI, BPI, and BPM over the last few years, it is hardly surprising that there is no clear vision of what tomorrow will bring. It's probably safe to say that nobody will settle debates between IBM, Microsoft, Sun, and other technology giants any time soon, but beyond this, the odds of being able to describe the exact technology landscape of five or ten years from now are probably longer than those of an individual winning the Powerball jackpot.

So how do companies go about preparing for this unknown territory? In some ways this is a trick question. Companies should not necessarily spend their time preparing for the unknown; instead, they should focus on what they can predict. They may not know whether .NET will become the pervasive industry standard, for example, but they can be certain that ten years from now there will still be a need for integration technology, regardless of whether it is labeled BPI, BPM, or something entirely different. They can be assured, too, that flexibility and business agility will be as important tomorrow as they are today, or perhaps even more so. Companies can also count on standards continuing to evolve, new technologies being introduced, and the capabilities of existing technology growing more impressive. It is also extremely likely that interchangeable pieces – business activity monitoring, workflow, and modeling tools – will be critical to the success of integration projects.

This is not completely unlike high school seniors heading off to college with an undeclared major and no clear plan for a future career. These students may not have a clear vision of their professional landscape after they graduate, but they nonetheless are preparing for the future by getting an education that will later prove to be invaluable. Chances are these students will try to prepare by taking a wide variety of classes and gaining exposure to multiple disciplines, which will help as they make the transition from college to the working world.

## Survival of the Fittest

As companies brace for the difficult years ahead, they are more keenly aware of the competition than ever before. They know success depends on their ability to evolve and adapt to whatever changes the market demands. They cannot afford to stand idle and hope they will be the first to capitalize on some sort of unforeseen technology revolution; they must have some plans for integration.

Looking ahead, it seems clear that BPI offers a course for continuing evolution that minimizes risk while allowing companies to demonstrate incremental progress with predictable results. It is highly likely that the point-to-point approach to integration will all but disappear. The inefficiencies and shortcomings of this tactic are well documented. A large portion of businesses have experienced these limitations first-hand and have no desire to relive them. Certainly it is hard to imagine a future CIO announcing this as the company's ongoing "IT strategy." It is far more likely that companies will choose between trying to build an integration infrastructure or adopting business process integration.

We have described why building an integration infrastructure is a difficult proposition, and there are no signs that this will get any easier. We *know* technologies and standards will evolve, so the pieces of the stack will change continually, and companies will need to devote significant time to making the various layers interact seamlessly, just as they do today.

But even companies that have not settled on a specific approach can make progress, as long as they remain focused on integration in general. A company does not have to purchase a BPI product to do its integration homework. Every company, large or small, should be devoting time to understanding its integration pain points. Companies need to know the root cause of manual handoffs and inefficient processes, just as they need to understand their competitive strengths and weaknesses. They should be able to identify projects that will deliver ROI, cut costs, or allow them to carve a new niche in the marketplace. Further, they should be able to slice these projects into manageable increments and identify solutions that can be reused throughout the enterprise.

A company that has given thought to potential projects is in an enviable situation. Most BPI vendors today are more than willing to do proofs of concept or pilot projects because they are confident that, after seeing the product in action, prospects will realize the possibilities BPI offers. Companies should take advantage of these opportunities; the reward of dramatic business improvement in exchange for dedicating resources to a pilot for a week or two is well worth the risk. Consider the success story we described earlier that involved streamlining credit card processing; this short, self-contained integration project had a ripple effect throughout the entire state organization because the credit card functionality was used in so many business processes. Likewise, the company that used BPI to provide real-time responses to an independent agency's quote requests suddenly had the wherewithal to do so with *any* agency, including agencies with which they were not currently doing business.

Businesses can make progress today and be confident that they are heading in the right direction, even if they do not know where the technology path will ultimately take them. Companies can realize business benefits by embracing emerging standards like Web services without locking themselves in or betting too heavily on any one standard. Instead of Web service-enabling every application for the sake of standardization, businesses can use BPI to take advantage of Web services where it has the greatest impact to customers or opens a partner channel that otherwise would remain closed.

A company that has begun to make the transition to a process-centric organization has a clear advantage over an organization that still focuses on how it will move data from system to system. Once a company starts down the process-centric path, it will never look back. If a company confronts its integration problems in the right fashion – by facing them head on with the appropriate set of tools and the right approach – the myriad applications that appeared to be the very source of the trouble will be transformed into the invaluable assets they were always intended to be.

# Glossary

Words appearing in **boldface** in the definitions are also defined in this glossary.

**ACORD (Association for Cooperative Operations Research and Development)**
A nonprofit insurance association with a mission to facilitate the development and use of standards for the insurance and related financial industries.

**adapter**
Also known as a **connector**, an adapter is a software component that serves as an interface between an IT system and an integration engine.

**API (Application Programming Interface)**
Businesspeople access system functionality through user interfaces; developers access system functionality through APIs.

**application server**
System software designed to host business applications. Application servers simplify the task of application development by isolating applications from the operating system and taking over connectivity, memory management, runtime execution, **scalability**, and **failover**.

**B2Bi (Business-to-Business Integration)**
Computer-to-computer communication between two or more businesses.

**back-end system**
Type of application, program, or system that processes or stores information behind the scenes. Users typically do not interface directly with back-end systems; they work with **front-end** systems.

| | |
|---|---|
| **BAM (Business Activity Monitoring)** | The monitoring of business processes in real time via specialized tools that help companies react to runtime errors or identify processing bottlenecks. |
| **BPI (Business Process Integration)** | Software that allows a company to automate its business processes that involve multiple, incompatible systems. For some detail on this concept, read the rest of this book. |
| **BPM (Business Process Management)** | BPM is frequently used interchangeably with **BPI**, but in the industry there are also definitions that consider BPM a superset of **BPI** that includes **workflow**, **BAM**, and reporting functionality. |
| **bus (also known as a message bus)** | Software that allows an application to communicate with (send messages to and from) and make requests of other applications without knowing who will be "answering." |
| **Business Process Reengineering** | A methodology in which a company revisits and analyzes its business processes to determine how to make them more efficient. The concept generally emphasizes extreme change and often results in recommendations to rebuild the processes from scratch. |
| **buzzwords** | Also know as "techno babble," buzzwords are words or acronyms that few truly understand, and some of which make no sense at all, but nonetheless make the speaker sound sophisticated and technically savvy. An example of a buzzword-compliant sentence might be, "Morphing leading-edge paradigms to seize enterprise methodologies helps to cultivate viral architectures and embrace collaborative bandwidth." |

## Kiss the Frog

**CIO (Chief Information Officer)** — The C-level executive in a company who is responsible for leadership of the company's IT department, and the person who will be blamed if he or she chooses the wrong approach to integration technology.

**COM (Component Object Model)** — Microsoft's strategic building-block approach to developing computer applications.

**connector** — Same as an **adapter**.

**CORBA (Common Object Request Broker Architecture)** — Often confused with a poisonous snake native to Africa and Asia, CORBA is a standard architecture and specification for allowing programs developed by different vendors to communicate through an "interface broker."

**CRM (Customer Relationship Management)** — The programs and methodologies a business uses to manage its customer information in ways that allow the business to organize and exploit the information to its best advantage.

**data transformation** — Changing the format of data from one system to accommodate the required format of another.

**data-centric** — A traditional approach to integration that focuses primarily on moving data back and forth between incompatible systems. BPI promotes a **process-centric,** rather than a data-centric, approach to integration.

**distributed application** — Any application that executes on more than one computer. With this type of application, business operations can be conducted from any geographical location.

| | |
|---|---|
| EAI (Enterprise Application Integration) | The traditional way in which a company attempts to achieve integration through the implementation of infrastructure software, typically with a data-centric approach. |
| EJBs (Enterprise JavaBeans) | Sun Microsystems' component model for developing and deploying Java objects for **distributed applications**. |
| ERP (Enterprise Resource Planning) system | A single, large (typically multi-million dollar) application that is intended to provide all a company's software needs, such as **CRM**, **SCM**, inventory control, and more. |
| failover | Activation of a secondary, often redundant component that allows a system to remain fully functional when the primary component becomes unavailable (because of power loss, scheduled down time, etc.) |
| fault-tolerant | A fault-tolerant computer system is designed so that, if one component fails, a backup component can take its place immediately with no adverse effect on end users. |
| front-end system | An application with which a user interacts directly. Front-end systems are usually supported by **back-end** systems. |
| gateway | A point on a network acting as the entry point to another network. Gateway is often synonymous with **portal**. |
| geek | A person who reads technical glossaries. |
| green screen | A text-only computer screen that is driven by keyboard commands, rather than a mouse, scroll bars, and drop-down menus. |

## Kiss the Frog

| | |
|---|---|
| GUI (Graphical user interface) | A "point-and-click" user interface that is driven by visual elements, such as scroll bars, buttons, icons, and other images, rather than purely text-oriented commands. |
| high availability | A system with high availability is one that functions effectively regardless of increases in user demand or machine failure. |
| IT (information technology) | A term used to describe broadly all kinds of technologies that involve moving, storing, exchanging, and using data. |
| J2EE (Java 2 Platform, Enterprise Edition) | A Java platform designed by Sun Microsystems and its partners to simplify the grand-scale kinds of computing typically done by large corporations. |
| legacy application | An application that has been around for awhile and usually serves its purpose well, but does not collaborate with newer systems because it was not built using current technology. Legacy applications are usually too expensive to replace and need to be integrated with other applications to automate business processes. |
| load balancing | The act of distributing work among computers so processing takes less time and users are served more quickly. |
| message broker | A program that translates a sender's message, in its formal **messaging** protocol, to the receiver's formal **messaging** protocol. |
| messaging | A method of communication between software components or applications in which the sending component and receiving component do not have to be available at the |

| | same time or know of each other's existence. |
|---|---|
| metadata | Information about or a description of data. |
| middleware | A general term for any programming that glues together two or more applications. Middleware usually includes **messaging** services so that the different applications can communicate. |
| packaged application | Companies purchase a packaged application when they don't want to develop an application on their own. In the case of integration technology, companies purchase packaged **BPI** applications when they don't want to build an integration infrastructure on their own or develop point-to-point solutions. |
| portal | A business's portal is a comprehensive collection of functionality (usually powered by multiple **back-end** applications) that a user can access through a single **front-end**. It is not the same as Yahoo, Google, or other Web portals that serve as a single Web site from which users can access many other Web sites. |
| process modeling | Designing in a graphical environment a representation of a business process, including the order of the individual steps that make up the overall process. After the design is complete, process models are converted into executable programs. |
| process-centric | An approach to integration that focuses primarily on business processes and company objectives, as opposed to traditional **data-centric** approaches that focus primarily on the movement of data between applications. |

## Kiss the Frog

**runtime engine** — The component of an integration technology solution that allows processes to be executed. The runtime engine coordinates the activity that occurs between the incompatible systems that take part in an automated process.

**SCM (Supply Chain Management) system** — An SCM system integrates internal company resources to manage and work effectively with external suppliers. SCM systems generally focus on manufacturing capability, market responsiveness, and customer-supplier relationships.

**STP (Straight-Through Processing)** — The ability of a system to execute a process from start to finish without manual intervention.

**UML (Unified Modeling Language)** — A standard notation that unifies three earlier object-oriented design and analysis methodologies and that is used to model real-world objects and to communicate about the models.

**Web services** — Essentially, **APIs** for the Internet. They allow functionality to be accessed over the Internet, and like other **APIs**, do not have user interfaces.

**workflow** — Automation of business processes during which documents, information, or tasks are passed from one human participant to another, according to defined business rules.

**XML (Extensible Markup Language)** — An easily adaptable way to create and share common information formats and data widely and consistently – for example, on the Internet.

# Author's Biography

## Richard Schultz

"Integration should not be this hard," says Richard Schultz, who decided to tackle the challenge head-on by founding Metaserver, Inc., in 1996. In just a few years this innovative entrepreneur has seen his company, which develops business process integration (BPI) software, grow from a staff of three in borrowed office space to a fifty-five-person leading-edge technology firm located in the heart of downtown New Haven, Connecticut.

Fond of drawing parallels to computer networking – an industry with which Schultz is very familiar, having been exposed to technology development at large, leading-edge Fortune 500 Companies early in his career – Schultz points out that technology advances in the networking arena have revolutionized the role of network administrators. "Can the average person set up a network?" Schultz asks. "Probably not, but today, as opposed to twenty years ago, many people can. BPI tools will simplify software integration in the same way and put it within reach of many more companies."

While other young businesses were shutting their doors after the economic downturn of the early 2000s, Schultz's company used his entrepreneurial, managerial, and technical vision to develop an integration solution targeted primarily for the mid-market and suitable for the lagging economy. Metaserver's BPI software enables quick, cost-effective implementations and allows companies to demonstrate immediate return on investment. Recognized as *Business New Haven's* 2002 "Innovator of the Year" for raising venture capital and inspiring investor confidence in a climate unfriendly to most Connecticut businesses, Schultz attributes his success in part to the ability to make customers innovators. By taking advantage of Metaserver's solution to tackle complex business problems, such as real-time carrier-agent

## Kiss the Frog

integration in insurance, customers with tight budgets and a relatively fixed IT staff can keep pace with much larger competitors, while attaining greater agility.

Those who have known Schultz since his college days – when he earned the nickname "What If?" for consistently challenging ideas and looking for new ways to solve problems – aren't surprised that he ended up founding and running his own company. In earlier positions Schultz wrestled with complex, large-scale integration issues. Recognizing that large integration projects were often too slow-moving, he noted, "The same good ideas could be on the white board for five years." Schultz knew there had to be a simpler solution – not only for large enterprises, but also for mid-market companies that cannot afford solutions that take a year or more to implement.

At Metaserver, as at Schultz's previous companies, there is no shortage of innovative ideas, but the pace is faster, and the company is focused on helping customers solve real-life problems that range from allowing trucking companies to pay tax bills over the Internet to helping insurance companies work with independent agencies that have different systems and technology. Unlike many of his peers, Schultz has an ultimate vision of success that is not measured by having thousands of employees. He points to Metaserver as an example of a collection of entrepreneurial groups that function as one effective entity without being limited by structure and hierarchy. According to Schultz, "Success is having customers use our product in new and innovative ways and making money for the investors who helped get us started."

How does Schultz define innovation? "There are many different ways to be innovative," he says. "Sometimes innovation can be as simple as finding a unique way to reuse something or thinking about a problem in a different way. You can be innovative without being crazy or pie-in-the-sky." How does he recognize other innovative thinkers? "If people agree with everything I say, I start to wonder," he jokes. But Schultz is quick to add that it never hurts to ask, "What if?"